To Krista

Best of luck with
your clients

Philip Van Tuyl

8/18/11

Companies Are Talking ...

Whether your company is privately held, publicly traded or government owned or indeed a partnership between these interests, the laws of business economics are the same. Philip Varley achieves the remarkable feat of combining clear insights into these laws with hard-earned practical experience of corporate turnarounds, and does so in a most readable and gripping way.

> Michael Gerrard, CEO
> Partnerships UK, plc

Failure Is Not An Option will cause you to rethink the financial structuring of your business. Philip Varley has provided a tenacious recipe for successful turnarounds.

> Jerry F. Schmidt, Founder and Managing Partner
> Cordova Ventures

Philip Varley is one of those rare executives, unafraid to break crystal when needed. His refreshing style of directness is coupled with an intellect of identifying the crucial and timely actions that ensure success. This book shows you how to overcome current business obstacles and achieve that elusive, profitable growth in today's economy.

> Denny Chrismer
> VP Sales, Lockheed Martin Coherent Technologies

I hired Philip as Interim CFO during a time we were preparing for the sale of our private equity-owned manufacturing company. Philip was outstanding in that role. He stepped right in on short notice and we did not miss a beat operationally. As well, Philip did a great job assembling data needed for our marketing process. Top notch guy.

> Dave Smith, CEO
> Buddy's Kitchen, Minnesota

FAILURE
IS NOT
AN OPTION

FAILURE
IS NOT
AN OPTION

THE 12-STEP PLAN
TO SUCCESSFUL
TURNAROUNDS

PHILIP G. VARLEY

**mile high
press**

Publishers: Mile High Press, Ltd. and The Barrington Group, Inc.
www.MileHighPress.com, PO Box 460880, Denver, CO, 80046
www.TheBGI.com, 1 Mountain Cedar Lane, Littleton, CO 80127

Books may be purchased in quantity and/or for special sales by contacting the
publisher or author through the website www.MileHighPress.com,
at email address MileHighPress@aol.com, PO Box 460880, Aurora, CO, 80046,
or by contacting your local bookstore.

Cover and Layout Design: Nick Zelinger, NZ Graphics
Editing: Judith Briles (The BookShepherd) and John Maling (Editing By John)

Philip G. Varley FCA
    Failure Is Not an Option—The 12-Step Plan to Successful Turnarounds

Library of Congress Control Number: 2011921737

ISBN-13: 9781885331373

10 9 8 7 6 5 4 3 2 1

1. Business 2. Turnarounds 3. International Business

Printed in Canada

To the late John Hudson, Principal of my junior school, whose dedication to math teaching inspired my lifelong passion for numbers.

Acknowledgements

The seed of an idea for this book was planted five years ago by the CEO of one of my clients. We had together doubled the profitability of a manufacturing company and were in the middle of selling it for its Private Equity Group owners. As the CEO introduced me to the executives of one of the buyout partners, he described my role as "coming into a company with my own 12-step plan" to improve its efficiency.

I had not thought of what I did as following a game plan up to that point, but on review of how I had enhanced profits in other companies, I realized that I always followed the same plan, with different degrees of emphasis depending on whether the company was a manufacturer or service provider, domestic or international, large or small.

After we sold that company, I began the outlines of this book, but no sooner had I begun to write, I became involved in two more turn-arounds. These provided some more examples of how to wring blood out of a stone, and when they were complete I sat down in earnest to capture all the relevant vignettes. As more than half of the companies I have been involved with were facing imminent bankruptcy when I was brought in, I decided to give the book an appropriate title, because if those companies had not returned to profitability, the results would have been disastrous. Hence, with all due respect and thanks to Eugene Kranz, Flight Director of Apollo 13, the title chosen for the book was *Failure Is Not An Option.*

A number of people must be recognized for their assistance with the completion of this book. In academia, Professor Ron Reed of the Monfort College of Business, University of Northern Colorado, has been tireless in providing me with entrees to guest lecturing at different schools. Those lectures all provided feedback for altering the emphasis on a particular topic. And thanks to Ron Rizzuto at the Daniels College of

Business at the University of Denver for involving me with his turnaround module in the entrepreneurship program.

Once the book was written, editorial assistance came from Michael Gerrard, Mike West, Joe Adams and Al Valenti. And my good legal friend, John Eckstein, probably put more marks on the manuscript than anyone else, even though he was not billing for his time!

Given that the main premise of the book is that successfully turning around a business is akin to successfully landing a plane, no matter what hazards mother nature throws at you, special thanks must go to the first flight instructor who was able to teach me to land, Matt Schroeder. Without his perseverance, I would never have enjoyed the more than 1200 hours of flying I have experienced flying hundreds of times over the Colorado mountains. Matt now has the best possible window office, flying jets from coast to coast.

Finally, to my publisher, Judith Briles, who was a speaker at a professional group I belong to, and whose subject was that everyone "had a story." She listened to mine, and this is the result!

Table of Contents

Introduction

What Will You Accomplish By Reading "The 12-Step Plan" And Why Do You Care?

By reading this book and implementing its strategies, you will see at least a 10 percent improvement in your company's gross margins.

Why Did I Write This Book?

The answers are straightforward. I have performed numerous successful turnarounds in a global arena and the companies which have benefited from my services have shared common negative characteristics. The industries those companies were engaged in are irrelevant to these characteristics. This book identifies the commonalities found in all of these underperforming companies and tells you exactly what to do in your own company to capture those savings and improve its profitability.

During my career, I have been shocked at how little fiscal control has been exercised at small and mid-sized companies, and in a number of cases, really large publicly traded companies as well. As a result of this lack of fiscal control, most companies' profits have been far smaller than they might otherwise have been.

What this lack of control means for companies which are operating profitably is that in the short term the owners have been shortchanged, and in the longer term, there are fewer financial reserves than there might otherwise be for riding out economic storms.

For those companies currently operating at a loss, unless they implement some of the measures in this book, their days are numbered—traditional funding sources of lending and equity have dried up. Most lenders today are lending to companies only with positive cash flow.

The fact that you are reading *Failure Is Not An Option* means that you recognize that poor performance must be changed. If your company has a revenue stream, it is probably viable. If your revenues are above $30 million per year, multiple consumers have clearly demonstrated that you have a winning product in the market place and as a result, the only reason for your company to fail is because you have failed to keep expenses below the level of revenues.

I am often challenged on this extremely simple observation: that with $30 million or more of revenues, the only reason for failure is lack of cost control. But let me demonstrate why this is true. For expenses to exceed revenues, it must cost more to produce a product than that item is sold for. If managements approve such a strategy, it means one of two things: Either they have no knowledge of their cost structure (a large number), or they are in fact aware of their cost structure but choose not to make what they perceive to be the hard and unpleasant decisions necessary to bring the company back to profitability (the vast majority). This is frequently the case in long-lived, family firms, where revenues have declined over time, where staff are regarded as members of the family, but their numbers have not been reduced appropriately to meet diminished needs.

I will demonstrate as *Failure Is Not An Option* progresses, that there is no reason to fear making these decisions. Keeping a company alive preserves the jobs of those remaining with the company. Allowing a company to fail, forces everyone—the bad *and* the good—out onto the streets. Allowing the hard working and efficient to lose their jobs because of a failure of management to identify and eliminate the poor performers is an abrogation of management responsibility.

By following the recommendations in this book, many reductions in workforce will be made by the employees themselves as they realize that a well-managed, efficient environment is not one in which they want to spend their days. And the good performers will be encouraged to even higher levels of achievement as they realize that there is no longer any room for freeloaders.

During my turn-around career, I have had to reduce staffs, sometimes significantly. But it has only been very rarely that I have actually had to fire anyone. Almost all the attrition was voluntary, from people who realized that under my management, they would no longer be able to hitch a free ride. The secrets to encouraging people to see that they should seek pastures new, will be found in Chapter 3, *The Organization Chart du Jour* and Chapter 4, *Zero Tolerance for Error*.

There are many people whose political beliefs are opposed to firing anyone, but under any economic system there is a limited amount of cash available to fund those jobs. By eliminating deadwood, I have enabled my client companies to remain viable, in business, and employing probably four times as many people as were terminated. If these companies had not been brought back to profitability, then the only other option would have been for these companies to declare bankruptcy, with the loss of *all* positions.

While excessive salary costs are usually the main driver of lack of profitability, regular expenses in these companies frequently get out of hand for the same reasons that staffing does. "Managers" seem to be engaged in popularity contests and don't like to be seen "controlling" others. Frequently when policies and procedures are introduced to min-imize expenses, for example for purchasing office supplies or travelling on business, gripes from the trenches will be heard. The common theme of these push-backs is along the lines of "you hired me but by introducing this policy you are showing you don't trust me." Well, President Reagan was famous for the quote: "trust, but verify."

Travel expenses are described in Chapter 6, *Travel and Entertainment— Yes!*, as they are an area of business where the same amount of business can be accomplished for 50 percent less simply by planning ahead. In most cases, these expenses are egregious because everyday employees are often not aware of the multiplicity of travel pricing options and yield manage-ment systems used by travel companies, and how they can fight back by tailoring their behavior to take advantage of these opportunities.

Manufacturing companies have been well represented in my turn-arounds. Almost overnight, costs in these companies can be reduced by 20 percent. In distribution, the same percentage holds true. Within six months to a year, there will usually be the opportunity to reduce manufacturing costs by an additional 20 percent, by the implementation of Demand Flow Technology to design an efficient production line.

Companies specializing in consulting services offer a separate challenge, as the output per employee is more difficult to measure, but here, cost control is achieved by applying the concepts of job profitability and project accountability, and these then become the hallmarks of a successful team leader.

When American companies enter the international arena, the two documents which are the hallmark of *Failure Is Not An Option*, the *Organization Chart du Jour* and the *13-Week Cash Flow Forecast*, together with a full year budget, are absolutely critical to ensuring that you are not taken for a ride by a group of people 5,000 miles away who often see the US owner as an unlimited ATM. In addition, a thorough understanding of local tax laws and corporate structure can by itself enable far more money to be repatriated from even the most inefficient subsidiary than from one which is unplanned, or planned assuming local laws mirror those of the US. Chapter 13, *TurnArounds in the International Arena* provides some ideas on how to raise profitability abroad, by among other things, a thorough understanding of foreign tax laws.

The fact that you are reading *Failure Is Not An Option* demonstrates that you care enough about your company, its shareholders and employees. By the time you have finished it, you will be ready to embark on your own 12-step plan, and will marvel at how much hidden profit you have been able to discover, right under your feet!

A Turbulent Beginning

"Autopilot out of control, autopilot out of control" is what brought home to me the severity of the storm that had without warning engulfed me and my little plane, a Cessna 182 enroute from Salina, Kansas, to Centennial Airport, Denver.

What should have been an uneventful three hour flight on autopilot, level at 8,000 feet, in stratus clouds and under the watchful eyes of air traffic controllers, had suddenly been thrown into disarray with tornadic winds tossing me this way and that, and hail, thunder and lightning providing additional dramatic effect.

"Say altitude," the unemotional air traffic controller called—a polite way for the FAA to remind pilots on instrument flight plans that they have deviated from their assigned altitude—a bit naughty when you are flying in clouds and are relying on controllers to keep you separated from other traffic flying equally blindly in the clouds.

"Thirteen thousand, 4,000 feet per minute updraft, thunderstorm," was my response as I pulled the throttle back to idle and became hyper-active at interpreting the instruments to figure out which way was up and avoid a fatal dive from excess speed, or a stall and spin from flying too slowly.

"Cleared any altitude, any heading, suggest turn left 150 (degrees), IF ABLE," intoned the controller, calmly. It was his "if able" that caught my attention. I knew that meant he realized I was in a bad way, but I also knew from what I was experiencing and the "if able," that I was going to have to be very careful in getting out of this one, the closest I have come to failing to perform a turn-around successfully!

But I also knew that if I followed the basic rules of the game, I had a very good chance of exiting the other side intact, because planes are built to withstand extremes of turbulence, if they are treated with respect. That means keeping them right side up, and within an envelope of speed that is neither too slow nor too fast. I have taught aviation students, and the first fear they have to eliminate from their minds is that turbulence does not break planes; rather, it is pilots' *reactions* to turbulence which leads to their crashing. Likewise, in business, companies don't just happen to fail, it is when their executives lose control that the death spiral begins.

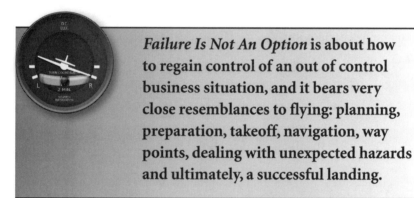

Failure Is Not An Option **is about how to regain control of an out of control business situation, and it bears very close resemblances to flying: planning, preparation, takeoff, navigation, way points, dealing with unexpected hazards and ultimately, a successful landing.**

Back in the clouds, I was being tossed around like a cork on a rough sea. I was focusing intently on the attitude indicator and airspeed. It was critical that I kept us right side up, and the speed between 80 and 110 knots. At one point, due to the violence outside, we entered the red zone, meaning there was a possibility the plane would break up due to outside forces exceeding design limitations, but I was able to recover.

This required all my learned skills and training to kick in—from auto-pilot to "auto-brain." When I was finally able to be wings level, and slowed down, it was time to look at the altitude (the ground was at an elevation of about 5,000 ft.), and then see if I was able to turn left to 150 degrees, as the controller had suggested a few minutes earlier.

What saved me and my passenger? I had two things going for me in this turnaround situation, both of which were the result of good planning and risk management. First, I had no worries about deadlines, or running out of reserves (fuel), and second, I was focused on a successful outcome, getting back on the ground. In the infamous words of Eugene Kranz (Apollo 13 Mission Controller), "failure was not an option." Provided I could keep us right side up, we could be banged about for another four hours. And I knew that spring storms rarely lasted four hours, nor covered areas of more than 400 miles in every direction at the same time.

The four hours and 400 miles were the capability I had from my fuel reserves. While the FAA mandates that for an instrument flight, a pilot put on enough fuel for the flight plan plus an extra 45 minutes of reserves, I have always believed that 45 minutes is not enough time to fly your way out of trouble if you are in the clouds when something goes wrong. I therefore always choose to put enough fuel on to get me to my destination and then back to where I started should something go wrong at the end. I assume that if I am able to take off at my origin, later, if weather deteriorates at the destination, I should be able to return and land back where I took off, or, I will find some clear weather within another 400 miles.

With the comfort of knowing that the storm would ultimately pass, all I had to do was get out of it, and once in calmer air, either wait it out until Centennial Airport itself was clear, or find an alternate destination. At the time, I didn't know that I had entered an embedded thunderstorm at level six, the most severe possible. Due to the climate, it had popped up without warning, and with the FAA's antiquated radar system at the time, it would not appear on their scopes for another six minutes after it had formed. Inexperienced pilots in those situations are in extreme jeopardy ... as are inexperienced executives—when the financial storm hits their companies.

For the company executive, reserves usually are perceived to mean cash, and it is usually the lack of such reserves that causes the immediate storm. And while most executives think that the crisis just pops up on them, as my embedded thunderstorm did, that is not usually the case. What is usually true is that they don't see it popping up because they have failed to project their company's path into the future.

After 20 minutes of intense battering, (so severe that after I finally landed, I actually looked at my plane for dings and dents), I was out of the clouds, out of the hail and the lightning, but now with a different hazard. I was in the gust front, and between cloud layers. That meant I had an undercast below me, an overcast above, and was being battered by winds surrounding the storm. But at least I could see, and to the south-west of me was Pikes Peak, a 14,000 foot mountain in the Colorado Rockies. After enquiring about my fuel reserves and realizing I was adequately prepared for what mother nature could throw at me, ATC directed me to fly toward Pikes Peak and hold (keep circling) in the clear air nearby. The storm currently raging over Centennial was moving northeast at about 10 mph. The assumption was that within the hour we would be able to land there.

While this appeared to be good news, the late hour meant that it was going dark, and the temperature was dropping to below freezing. My plane was not certified for flight into known ice. But Centennial was my home airport, I had flown the instrument approach many times, and most recently (the previous weekend), I had performed multiple practice approaches with a flying buddy, so I was confident I could get in, even with visibility down at "minimums," at Centennial Airport, a cloud ceiling just 200 feet above the ground. And because the temperature increases by three degrees Fahrenheit for every 1000 feet of descent,

I knew that as I descended on the approach, any ice which I might have encountered earlier should melt off before landing.

After what seemed like an eternity, ATC deemed the storm over Centennial to be sufficiently far away to clear me for the approach, which meant climbing back into the clouds to join the localizer (guidance to the runway). Once over the final approach fix, and into the descent, I just kept looking for the rabbit (white lights racing toward the runway end) and finally, 200 feet above ground, I saw the runway. Momentarily, I thought I was home and dry until I realized that there was still torrential rain coming down and this landing was going to be slippery.

Concentration and focus flying the plane back onto the deck brought me down on the centerline. With adrenaline pumping I taxied to the hangar. It took another day before my legs stopped shaking.

What a Successful Flight in Extreme Turbulence Can Teach a Company Executive

Executives and pilots have a great deal in common. What can you, an executive in charge of a company, learn from this flight into the unknown?

Planning

The flight had been planned to take three hours at an altitude of 8,000 feet in smooth stratus clouds. I knew how long the flight should take, because I had a detailed flight plan. Companies need to know how long their turnaround will take by having a week-by-week cash budget.

Preparation and Plotting a Course

I had studied the charts, and as I was flying IFR (instrument flight rules) my road map in the sky was plotted with precision. The weather forecast was for stable conditions—a layer of stratus clouds at my chosen altitude all the way. Even though the plan only called for a three hour flight, I had put enough fuel on board for seven hours, because in the event of an unexpected instrument failure, I wanted to be able to find clear weather and it is rare not to find clear weather somewhere within 400 miles of where you are! I had carefully performed my airplane's preflight check on the ground, and everything had worked.

In the corporate world, the "weather forecast" is the macro-economic forecast. The flight plan is the budget, the fuel to meet budget is the staff, and the reserve fuel is real cash to take care of emergencies. Too many companies are flying on fumes—relying for needed cash flow on potential sales from a "pipeline report." Companies MUST have adequate fuel on board.

Take-off

Because of thorough preparation, my takeoff went according to plan. In business as well, things don't just happen, someone needs to move the throttle forward and decide when to take action.

Navigation

I had my way points, paper charts and a moving map GPS. Every 15 minutes or so, I updated my progress, and compared it with the flight plan. Companies' budgets are their flight plans, and their way points are the monthly comparison with actual financial results. Any deviation from the plan must be explained and corrected for, or a new plan created. You do not want to be off course without understanding the reasons, or not know where your new course is taking you.

Expect the Unexpected

As Donald Rumsfeld, former Secretary of Defense, remarked, "There are unknown unknowns." When the excrement hits the fan, or in this case, the hail hits the propeller, you must be ready to act. Even though in an instant I had an unexpected crisis, because of preparation, I had plenty of fuel, and because of frequent checking of way points I knew exactly where I was in all three dimensions. As a result, I was IMMEDI-ATELY ready to deal with getting out of the crisis, without having to worry about finding out where I was or whether or not I had a time emergency to add to the weather. In a company, if you know your cash reserves, your staffing levels, your excess operations, your underperforming assets, if you suddenly suffer the loss of a major client, you can quickly evaluate the effect and take action immediately. You will survive.

Dealing with the Crisis

Engaging Resources

At the instant of crisis, ATC knew I had only one thing on my mind—keeping right side up. They cleared the area of other traffic so that I did not have to worry about other external constraints in terms of exactly where I could fly. Right then, my only concern was about flying. Where to is secondary. In a business, the only immediate concern for a company losing money means ensuring there is enough cash for payroll, because without employees, there is no company. Where you find that cash is irrelevant.

Not Losing Control

Provided I could stay right side up and within my speed envelope, I could stay alive indefinitely, or at least another four hours, which in those circumstances, was indefinitely! Likewise, in a company, provided you have brought your expenses down to match revenues, you can stay alive indefinitely, and take your time to decide how to grow once the crisis has passed.

Focus on the Outcome

Failure could be fatal. The only thing that mattered once I was in the storm was getting out of it alive. That's it. The time it took, where the ultimate landing site would be, or whether or not the plane would be damaged were irrelevant. Likewise with an imperiled company, whether or not it is battered at the end of the restructuring does not matter provided it has weathered the storm.

Successful Landing

Finally, once I had extricated myself from the storm, I had to make a successful landing. It would not have mattered if I had survived the storm and then crashed into the ground, or survived the crash but died in the fire, as is a pilot's favorite aphorism. The only focus was on a successful landing. For a company in trouble, that means handing over the reins to new owners, merging, selling the company, or learning new techniques to lead and manage the company into a new future.

Conclusion

This prologue described how a flight from Salina, Kansas, to Centennial, Colorado, could have been fatal when the heavens exploded, but planning, preparation, navigation, dealing with the crisis, engaging resources, not losing control, and focusing on the outcome, achieved a successful landing. Failure was NOT an option.

On an aircraft, the Captain and the First Officer are a team, and have been trained to not only complement the other, but perform the other's job in case of emergency. The Captain is the strategist; he plots the course, and ensures that the actions his crew take enable the plane to follow that course. His instrument panel tells him where he is, and his First Officer reviews that against the flight plan, making course corrections as necessary. At the end of the flight, both review the actual time elapsed, and fuel consumed against the plan, complete all the paperwork, and sign their log books.

In a corporation, the CEO and CFO are the flight crew, the CEO strategizes and the CFO puts together the corporate plan and operational budget. Periodically the actual financial results are compared to budget, and in many companies a "dashboard" of results, not unlike an airplane's instrument panel, is created to enable mid course corrections to be undertaken. At the end of the year, the books are closed, and an audit report is signed off!

When you, as the chief executives of your company have prepared for your company's opportunities and challenges, know where you are going, and have adequate training and reserves, you are well prepared to deal with whatever the economy can throw at you. Not only will you survive, you will thrive.

I think I'll change into something profitable.

CHAPTER 1

It's Always in the Numbers, Always!

The Key to It All—The 13-Week Cash Flow Forecast

You would think that turning around loss-making businesses would provide sufficient excitement for one person, but just in case it is not stressful enough, I spend my free time flying a small plane over the mountains as an instrument-rated commercial pilot. One of the privileges allowed by holding such a rating is the ability to "fly blind." That means I can fly my airplane in the clouds with no outside references to guide me. But this doesn't mean I don't know where I am or where I am going. I have a dashboard of instruments, from a very sophisticated Global Positioning System, which can show me exactly where I am with reference to ground features and weather systems, down to the old-fashioned basic "six-pack" of back-up analog instruments. They include, for example, heading and airspeed indicators which, together with navigation radios picking up electronic signals from distant beacons, can tell me where I am, my direction of travel, my altitude, speed, and which side is up!

In the clouds, trained pilots fly from point A to point B successfully by using all of the instruments on their dashboards, which provide them with real time data. They then compare these data with pre-planned and known references shown on their flight management systems, or, if doing it the old fashioned way, on paper print-outs such as flight plans drawn on navigation charts. The goal is that the actual position matches the expected position. In order to ensure that the pilot knows where he is along the way, if the pilot is flying in the clouds, the FAA mandates that he report his position to air traffic controllers through periodic compulsory "reporting points."

Non-pilots often believe that it is possible to fly a plane by the "seat of their pants," but as anyone knows who has ever flown in the clouds, or in a simulator set up to represent cloud flying, such feats are impossible. It only takes a few seconds in clouds to lose all reference to outside cues, and end up in a "death spiral," where the plane spins out of control before crashing into the ground.

I have found that the same beliefs exist in companies which get into trouble. Their executives are of the opinion that they can manage by the seat of their pants with no instruments or charts to guide them. The dashboards of instruments which would tell the executives their position are the actual weekly or monthly financial results. And the navigation charts telling them where they are expected to be and where they are ultimately going are the budget and forecast. Many CEOs believe that they can manage the business without accurate financial reports, and many CFOs feel they know their company's financial position "in their head." But without a frequent and periodic "compulsory reporting point," which for a company is the comparison of the budget with the actual financial results, they too are soon likely to descend into that death spiral, spin out of control, and enter bankruptcy.

Assuming that a pilot can keep his plane right side up and avoid mountains, the most important piece of information he needs to know to keep him in the air is fuel remaining. Assuming a CEO can make a product the market wants, the most important information he needs to know to keep the company afloat is *cash in the bank*!

The 13-Week Cash Flow Forecast

Please note: throughout this chapter I use the term "you" rather than "we," when describing a recommended course of action. However in Chapters 2 and subsequently in Failure Is Not An Option, *I use "we" versus "you" in relaying a strategy for turnaround success. When I do this, I will be describing a scenario where I am putting myself in as a team member for the example ... thus the "we."*

The key to managing all successful turnarounds is managing for positive cash flow. This is so important I will repeat it. You must make sure that overall, net cash is flowing in the door rather than out! And a Feng Shui expert can only do so much. Even profitable companies can go bankrupt when they don't have the cash required to pay the bills when they come due. The cash flow statement is the most important financial report that any company can ever produce. Just as the pilot in the clouds has to know his position at all times, the CEO must constantly know where his cash is.

Understanding your cash means more than just knowing what's in the bank today. It includes forecasting how much you will have at the end of this week. How much is your payroll total, how frequently is it paid, and on which days will the funds necessary to pay your staff be sequestered from your bank account? When is the next principal payment due on your loan(s)? Can you pay the rent?

For a pilot, for almost every situation he will perform in the cockpit, there is a checklist. Such checklists remind him what needs to be done every time he reconfigures the plane, climbs or descends, changes speeds, or meets with unexpected events. In the same manner, an organization must use a checklist to review its configuration as often as circumstances change. For a company in trouble, that could be as often as every day! But certainly a check must take place at least once each week. And the company's key checklist is the cash flow forecast.

 **The airline checklist is there for a reason: the Captain and First Officer work as a team to make sure each knows what the other has done. So in your company, make sure that the CEO and CFO work together as a team so that the CEO fully understands the financial situation of the company using the Cash Flow Forecast as a checklist.**

Hard as it is to believe, many companies don't accept that budgets, forecasts, or weekly financial reviews are of value. But if airlines have found that having two people review the configuration of a plane multiple times during the course of a flight ensures the successful outcome of that flight, wouldn't it also make sense that reviewing a company's cash position periodically during a month would enable it to more efficiently reach its desired outcome?

As of this writing, I have performed eight turnarounds. *Failure Is Not An Option* provides you with the facts about how each was saved from bankruptcy and was sold or became a successful stand-alone entity. The same fundamental problems were found in each, enabling the same methodologies to be applied in varying degrees to each of them to regain profitability, although the emphasis varied between them.

The most pervasive and egregious common factor among all eight of these troubled companies was that their executives had no idea of their true cash position. In fact, it usually came as an unpleasant surprise to them when they couldn't make a scheduled payment, or their bank or other outside investor pointed out their financial deficiencies through covenant violations or by calling in a note. In those companies, annual budgets were viewed as unnecessary administrative burdens. In one situation, the CEO claimed that because no one could predict changes to the macro economy, and with frequent technological advancements, his company's products might become obsolete as changes happened more and more rapidly in the future, why would they bother with creating a forecast which would need to be updated regularly?

Additional excuses often presented by executives who chose not to maintain strict financial control were that they trusted "everyone to do the right thing for the company," therefore, for example, critically reviewing expenses would be an affront to those other individuals. Other push-backs from requiring good financial management came from manufacturing, research or sales heads who feared a loss of power to an accounting group if "numbers were required for decisions." But when the receivers are waiting in the wings, and Chapter 11 does not mean you are in the middle of a book, all of a sudden financial first principles come into play. Because the first thing the administrator will be asking you for is a cash analysis.

In every one of the companies whose turnaround I managed, there was a lack of a 13-week cash flow forecast at the time of my appointment. In most cases, these companies did not have annual budgets. None of the management teams held meaningful financial reviews. Those who at least had a cursory review would ignore the writing on the wall and take no action. Their executives just "hoped" things would get better, the "economy would turn around," the large customer who was "just about to sign" would sign, or they'd "win the lottery." Yes, their chances of things improving if they continued without making any changes were as slight as the chances of their winning the lottery.

In some situations, I was called in to these troubled companies just as they realized they were headed into a brick wall. In others, it was very painful for the CEO, often a long term owner or second or third generation family member, to be told by me that they would be out of cash within a short period of time if no actions were taken to change their business management. But also, in most of these situations, there had not been a CFO, or if there was a CFO, he had not stood up to the CEO to explain how bad things were. Often, this situation was by design of the CEO, where the CEO had hired someone who would be a yes man, or by default where the CFO had figured out he would be shown the door if he attempted to implement controls. Therefore, for his own short term self interest, he kept quiet.

Regrettably, traditionally in the US in particular, proactive profit management by CFOs is rare; instead it is often the purview of a COO. This probably reflects the frequently held perception by American senior executives, bankers, recruiters and accounting and law partners, that the CFO's role is primarily that of chief compliance officer reporting how their companies have performed (past tense) by creating accurate historical profit and loss statements, and filing such reports with the SEC. My own view of a CFO's role is that it should be forward looking in terms of using the historical numbers as a springboard for identify-ing future profit improvement opportunities. This view was shaped by my training as a Chartered Accountant in the UK, where the breadth and depth of study into all aspects of business operations is as great as that undertaken in even the best MBA programs.

The most valuable CFO is one who is a key strategic player in the executive suite, one who is able to explain how the company WILL perform in the future based on contemplated actions, and a person who will "make the numbers happen." A good finance and account-ing department is a profit center in and of itself, because, by knowing the financial performance of every aspect of the business, the CFO can advise on where to invest, where to cut, which product or division is perform-ing and which isn't. Accounting staff can ensure debts from customers don't go bad, financing is obtained at the most competitive rates, and lowest cost purchasing deals are negotiated. The major value added to a company's bottom line by the finance function comes from ensuring a profitable future rather than simply reporting the past.

Companies whose culture perceives CFOs as historians rather than adventurers leave the company's accountants to toil laboriously to ensure that their historical statements accurately reflect past activities in accordance with GAAP. Instead of using the numbers to focus on growing the business profitably, they are just as doomed as the captain of the Titanic who at 23:40 on April 14, 1912, was able to send a telegraph letting the world know exactly where he was but had failed to adequately scan the horizon ahead for the iceberg which was about to sink his ship.

The cash flow forecast is the checklist— use it to identify when and where to save and invest.

As we said earlier, just as the cockpit crew in a plane is a team of Captain and First Officer, performing crew resource management and seamlessly transitioning back and forth between one another depending on the particular task at hand, so the team driving the corporation must consist of the CEO and CFO working together—each doing in concert what they do best.

Every CEO who wants to expand his company profitably must utilize the power of numbers. He should encourage the CFO to teach him, and accept the fact that the CFO probably has a better grasp of the overall, long-term financial impact of a decision than the CEO, who is more likely to be focused on the long-term strategic direction.

Every CFO who wants to make the transition from historian to adventurer—being part of a winning team rather than reporting on a defeat—must become proactive rather than reactive. He must understand the story the numbers are telling him so that he can use them to ensure a profitable outcome.

You CAN "make the numbers happen" by creating a 13-week cash flow forecast, and ensuring that it is adhered to. It requires keeping track of every incoming and outgoing cash payment, and taking whatever corrective actions are necessary whenever a deviation is noted. Just as the NASA Mission Control team at Houston was constantly monitoring every moment of Apollo 13's return to Earth, and making mid-course corrections, so must you constantly monitor the financial performance of your company and adjust for any variations from the plan.

Understanding the Value and Importance of the 13-Week Forecast in any Financial Situation

I first developed the 13-week cash flow forecast when I was a first year engineering student at Imperial College, London. Undergraduate education in England is different from that in America for a number of reasons. Firstly, most students arrive at university understanding the basics of the subjects they plan on majoring in, having focused on those subjects exclusively in their last 2 years at high school. In addition, most university courses are very intense, and the assumption is that students will be studying "full time," not spending 20 hours per week on part-time jobs. Consequently, most UK undergraduate degrees only take three years to complete, and in many cases, achieve levels of expertise sometimes only found in American master's degrees. At the everyday level, most UK students live in a university-provided residence hall (dorm), rather than renting private accommodation. Cars are usually disallowed, discouraged, or there simply is nowhere to park them. Overall, the financial status of a UK student tends to be somewhat less flush than his US counterpart.

In those days, I lived in one room and had an allowance of about £250 for each of three 10 week terms (trimesters). I knew what my rent fees were, how much my text books would cost, and the price of a

Tube (subway) season ticket. What was left had to provide me with student luxuries, a few records, (predecessors of CDs and iTunes!), pints of Guinness (the drinking age is 18 in the UK), and concerts.

Determining how many luxuries I could afford was simple. All I had to do was subtract from my allowance the fixed costs of rent, books and commuting, and apportion what was left among the other categories, then divide those amounts by the number of weeks per term. The answer told me how many pints of Guinness or other activities I could engage in. At the end of term, the process would be reviewed again for the next term.

There were a number of factors which made my student forecast easy. The first was that I had only one item of income every term, at the start of the term. The second was that I only had to forecast for me, and I was easy to control. I did not have any employees, so I did not need to communicate with others and ensure that they were on board with my policies!

Now fast forward to today's requirements. The principles of financial forecasting for corporations remain the same even if the sums are orders of magnitude greater and the variables significantly more complex. We must identify exactly when and where our money is going to come from and on what we would like to spend it, or in many cases, at least at the start of a turn around, on what we are forced to spend it.

What the Cash Flow Forecast Looks Like

At this point it would help the reader to look at the example Cash Flow Forecast found in Appendix 3. The example provided is a very simple, generic and anonymous spreadsheet, but the most important point to note is its format. The columns start with the current date and go into the future week-by-week for 13 weeks, and then continue by month for the rest of the year. The rows denote every item of income and expense, at whatever level of detail the creator desires.

By creating this spreadsheet in Excel, it becomes a real time "living" document because it can be updated every time a new piece of information is learned, a commitment is changed, staffing is reorganized, or a customer payment is received. If no material activities take place for a period of time, at the very least the forecast should be reviewed weekly and a summary of prior week's ACTUAL cash transactions entered. The past week should then be compared with what was expected to have happened, and the future forecast should be revised to take account of any changes made to the company's operations during the prior week or which are about to be made in the coming days.

In many cases, especially during the early stages of a turnaround, the forecast may need to be updated daily. Reasons for such frequent updating might include:

- Reflecting receipt of a large sum of money from a customer,

- A decision which has just been made which will have significant impact on the costs, or

- To incorporate some new knowledge which has just been ascertained regarding the business operations which differs from prior assumptions.

For a smaller company, the spreadsheet may enable every line item to be visible on its face. For larger companies, every line item might be supported by an underlying spreadsheet. For example, if a company has hundreds of sales from many customers, revenues on the front sheet may be one line item, while a sub-ledger might identify revenues by customer. However, in a company which has just a few multi-million dollar contracts, each customer's expected payment date might appear on the front sheet

Whatever the size of company, however, the spread sheet will provide its user with the most critical piece of information—how much cash will be available at the end of every week based on the current situation. If that cash balance is negative, in order for the company to survive into the following week, there are more decisions to be made, costs to cut, revenues to collect, or new sources of funds to be found.

Where to Start

In order to create a cash flow forecast, there are two choices. You can use zero-based budgeting, which assumes you are starting from scratch, and every item of revenue and expense will be based on assumptions, or you can use historical data, extrapolated.

Any Interim CFO brought in from the outside who is at the top of his game will be able to construct the cash flow forecast from first principles. The sources of his information will be the detailed general ledger and subsidiary ledgers such as receivables and payables. A good starting point from which to estimate the weekly costs is obviously the historical profit and loss statement (P+L).

In reality, a company in trouble is one where frequently controls and reports have been allowed to lapse, and it is possible that these historical reports do not even exist. In that case, source documents such as payroll, may be the only information available, and the cash flow forecast will have to be updated each time a new piece of information is discovered.

Zero-based budgeting is often the method used by start-up companies. However, most existing companies do not have the flexibility to start from scratch. In these companies, we are endeavoring to improve what we already have, so we will use historical financial statements as a starting point.

In extreme circumstances, the company may not even have rudimentary financial records. My most complex turnaround was one such company. Its shocking financial performance happened because it had been created from the merger of two insolvent companies, one of which had NO financial records, and the other had at best unreliable records. As I explained to the company's outside counsel on my second day on the job—this was the only turn-around I had experienced where I had absolutely no clue as to the magnitude of the problem! This was the one situation where I did have to start from zero-based budgeting. When I made my first payroll, that told me how much to budget every two weeks going forward, and, as Travel and Entertainment (T+E) reports were submitted, I had a good idea of the amount of "overspend" in that department, and so on!

Day 1:
Stop all payments pending review of validity.

The last example provides the best reason yet for your first edict when you arrive at your new challenge: "From this day forth, no check will leave this company without my signature." This may be varied for practical purposes to "No payment will be made without my review." But it means that you will sign or see every check, and all bank transfer requests. It has three beneficial effects.

The first one is primarily for your benefit. By signing every check you gain immediate knowledge of where the company is spending its resources, and more specifically, who is spending the company's resources. By seeing everyone's Travel and Entertainment (T+E) checks, you get a clear sense as to who is the budget traveler and who is living the high life. By looking at payroll, you see where the overtime is occurring. And by seeing the invoices for materials, you can see if prompt payment discounts are being taken.

The second—a huge benefit in the case of a company whose financial statements are spotty—is that it helps you create the cash flow forecast. Seeing exactly what is being spent by each department gives you early indications of who as an executive or an employee is going to be on your side as you change the culture from one of profligacy to one of profitability. Remember, you need a team to support you and they must believe that "failure is not an option." If I am being brought in as CFO rather than CEO, I always put my NASA Apollo 13 cap on the table and ask the CEO if he supports this ideal, because if he does not, one of us will have to leave.

The third benefit of signing every check is that everyone in the company now knows that someone else will be reviewing their purchases. This will stop frivolous waste, and will also provide you with an opportunity to apply your superior knowledge about pricing, purchasing, negotiation etc. to a whole range of expenditures in order to reduce them. You will see if there is nepotism in award of contracts, and whether certain suppliers are ones whom you know could be improved upon. By the urgency of the checks "needing" to go out today, you will soon see who is a planner and who just reacts to situations. Strategic planning is critical in ensuring the long term success of the company, but in the short term, a failure by sales executives to plan sales calls, or by the manufacturing VP to appropriately schedule deliveries, means wasted dollars.

Reviewing all checks and contracts will enable you to determine if charges for such items as insurance, vehicle costs, leases, audit fees etc. are appropriate given the size of the company. That will allow you to set your priorities when it comes to selecting a classification of expenses to focus on, after personnel numbers have been stabilized.

Mechanics of Building the Cash Flow Forecast

Ideally your starting point should be the most recent balance sheet. The vast majority of accounting systems in use today have the ability to produce an instantaneous balance sheet. In addition, you would like to see the last twelve months of profit and loss statements in order to create some averages for recurring expenses. Also you can look for trends, either long term or seasonal, which might affect how you can apply forecasting to those averages.

Once you have those documents in your possession, you can use the balance sheet to identify the following critical data points for inclusion in the cash flow forecast:

On the Asset Side:
1. Beginning cash—what we have today
2. Beginning customer receivables—our immediate source of new cash going forward

On the Liability Side:
1. Outstanding loans—and due dates for payment of interest and principal
2. Customer payables—and when they need to be paid

You need to decide how you want to aggregate or disaggregate expenses for management purposes. I have found that there are 12 or so major expense categories (which are discussed at length in coming chapters) and any number of minor ones.

For the cash flow forecast to be of greatest value, it must separately identify the major items of expense. The more detailed the expense disclosures are, the easier it is to determine the priority for controlling them. Sub-ledgers can further analyze generic categories of expense, such as providing salary by employee, purchases by supplier, or whatever else is necessary to identify how to best control an expense. Literally and visually, you will then see that financial success is "all in the numbers."

What the cash flow forecast will present to you in stark detail is the amounts you are spending at any point in time. It is forward looking. A monthly profit and loss statement (P+L) on the other hand loses its impact as a management tool because it is a historical document which looks *backwards* to an arbitrary fiscal period, and it includes various non-cash charges such as depreciation of fixed assets. Using a P+L to get where you are going could be compared with trying to drive your car along the road using the rear view mirror!

Here are the main differences between a Cash Flow Forecast and a P+L:

Cash Flow Forecast
- It estimates where you are going.

- It starts with where you are today and looks forward as many weeks or months as you wish.

- It only looks at what happens to cash. Without cash, companies fail, *even if they are profitable!*

- It looks at sources and outflows and their timing, based on the dates that checks will be received in the mail or when they have to be sent out, or when money will be automatically withdrawn from the bank account.

- It takes account of repayments of loan principal.

- It can be day specific. For example, if payroll goes out on a Thursday, you need to make sure you have cash in the bank the day before!

- It calculates end of day, end of week or end of month actual cash balances.

Profit and Loss Statement
- It ends at a point in the past, for example, the last month, and looks backwards at what happened during that historical period.

- It takes no account of cash. Revenues and expenses are allocated to time periods based on the portion relevant for that time period (accrual basis of accounting).

- On the income side, it can show a falsely good position because it will record as revenue any sale which has taken place, even if cash will not be forthcoming for many months. It ignores critical issues such as date of collections.

- On the expense side, it can under-report needed funds. For example, with regard to a loan, it might only show as expense the amount of interest accrued in that period, but will ignore when a repayment of principal becomes due.

- It provides no guidance towards the future.

- It includes depreciation of fixed assets, which is a non-cash charge that you can do nothing about, without telling you about capital outlays for new equipment.

From the above descriptions, you can see that in order to control what is happening at a company, the cash flow forecast is critical. Broken down as it is into weekly periods, it will show you the weeks during which there is a concentration of funding requirements—usually the week containing the month end will be most critical. This is frequently when banks will take their monthly principal and interest repayment, landlords will want their rent checks, and benefits providers expect their monthly premiums. Combine such a week with the coincidence of a bi-weekly payroll, or a semi-monthly payroll, and you have the ingredients for major cash flow problems.

The categories of expense which provide you with the most critical data on the face of the cash flow forecast will typically be the following, in order of magnitude (excluding manufacturing supplies, which might represent 40 percent or more of a manufacturing company's expenses):

- Salaries

- Overtime

- Benefits (broken further into medical, dental, vision, life)

- T+E (broken further into air, hotel, car, entertaining)

- Rent (by facility)

- Insurance (liability, theft, property, D+O, workers comp)

- Legal (by law firm or category of legal expense—corporate, patent, employee)

- Interest on debt

- Principal repayments

- Payables (broken into categories, e.g. manufacturing supplies, office expense, leases).

- Transportation (fuel, maintenance, license)

- Capital expenditure

- Taxes (payroll, property, sales, use, international)

- Audit

In manufacturing companies, supply chain mis-management and purchasing inefficiencies, besides badly negotiated prices, will often lead to excess and obsolete inventory which has to be written off, and will be the major cost, ahead of labor.

In distribution and transportation companies, vehicle operating costs will be the second most expensive cost, after labor.

After you have created your first cut at the forecast, you will have identified where you can obtain the best immediate Return on Investment

(ROI) in terms of cash saved compared with time involved to accomplish the savings.

How to Populate the Initial Expense Forecast

From summing up the last 12 months' P+L, and dividing by 52, you will be able to calculate approximate weekly expenses for every separate line item used in the P+L. At this stage, you probably do not want to go to every line item, but instead could group expenses by category. For example, "T+E" may be a sufficiently discrete sub-total for your cash flow forecast today, even though a couple of weeks from now, when you have had a chance to identify who is careful with and who is wasteful of corporate resources when they travel, you may want to break down T+E into its component elements of air, hotel, car and entertainment. Or, you may want to break it down by individual traveler.

Also, rather than just straight-lining the 52 week expenses, you may need to make some adjustments for seasonality. Perhaps there will be less travel around Christmas. Perhaps the power bill is more in winter in the north of the US and greater in summer in the south.

For some expenses, a monthly straight line estimate of their costs may be better suited for the cash flow forecast. Typical examples of these would be rents, automatic withdrawals by the bank for interest and principal on loans, payments to corporate credit cards or travel vendors, and lease payments for office equipment.

Some expenses may be annual, for example an audit fee, an insurance premium, or staff bonuses. It should be noted that if major changes are made to improve risk management of the firm, for example if a significant downsizing occurs, safety programs are introduced or higher deductibles are selected, an insurance premium credit might be obtained creating an immediate one-time benefit to cash flow (see Chapter 7, *Flying Under the Radar Screen*).

In addition, the cost of items of a capital nature should appear in the forecast at the time the expense is expected to be incurred (although if you are in a turnaround situation, unless there is a significant ROI justification for the capital expenditure, it should probably be deferred). And even if ROI can be justified for a capital investment, for short term cash preservation it is possible that it still may make better sense, for example, to continue paying higher maintenance fees on an old truck than buying a new one.

The Spreadsheet

Armed with this cash flow data, you are ready to begin creating your spreadsheet. It may help at this point to bookmark Appendix 3, *13-Week Cash Flow Forecast*, where an example spreadsheet is provided.

The columns of the spreadsheet should be headed by the title "Week Beginning." Monday is the best day for a week to begin on, as it provides five business days to take action following the data to be provided every time the cash flow forecast is updated.

Produce at least the first 13 columns by week. Then go out an additional nine months by month, so that you have a rolling, one-year forecast. You may want to add the next month (week 14 to 17) as weekly forecasts. As each week rolls by, the forecast is updated, and at the end of each month, another new month is added on at the end—13 months away.

The captions for the rows can be as sparing or as detailed as you like. However, the top line and the bottom line must be CASH! The top line is "beginning cash" on the first day of the week, the bottom line is "ending cash" for the following Friday at the close of business.

The top line, extreme left cell, represents the opening cash. It is the total of all the cash accounts from your most recent balance sheet. Cash, and details of how to reduce costs of cash management are found in Chapter 8, *Treasury Management*.

Having cash on hand is the starting point for all of your funding decisions. Without a positive number in this line, at any point in the future, your company is in trouble. Focus on keeping it positive and life will be good!

The next set of rows on the spreadsheet will focus on customer receivables. This is where your money will come from. It is yours, and you MUST collect it. Details of how to become a successful debt collector is provided in Chapter 2, *What's Yours is Yours.*

The level of detail in the spreadsheet regarding receivables will depend on the relative value of your receivables compared with your revenue stream. If you have thousands of clients who pay you just a few hundred dollars per transaction, it may make sense to simply calculate the average outstanding period of the receivables, and create a daily average of cash collected based on that time frame. If on the other hand, you have just a few very large customers, perhaps fewer than 50 in total, or if just the 50 largest represent 80 percent of your revenues, then each of them should be identified by name, the amount outstanding put in a column by their name, and the best estimate of when this will be collected made. This is done in order that the cash receipt can be entered against the client name in the week when it is expected to be received.

The goal of the spreadsheet is visibility for you, so you can see where the cash is coming from and where it is going. It will also act as an early warning system, enabling you to change course if you pay enough attention to what it is telling you.

Let me take you back to the flying illustration. My GPS system provides me with a great deal of data besides just telling me where I am and where I am going. One of the pages it offers is the "wind" page. By comparing ground speed with air speed, and the direction the plane is pointing compared with the direction it is traveling over the ground, this part of the GPS can calculate the direction and velocity of the wind. Under smooth flying conditions, the data displayed with each recalculation will vary only slightly from the last data point, but on one occasion when I was approaching a particularly steep sided mountain pass, the wind page began displaying wind speeds of 70 knots from different directions. This was the early warning, reinforced by the need for significant control forces to maintain "right side up." Using these data inputs, I decided to abort the attempt to cross the pass, and instead headed the long way round, down the valley and around the end of the ridge.

As a business executive, you should heed the early warnings that your cash flow forecast provides you, by changing course in terms of how much money you plan on spending, or being creative in garnering more.

Collections are the easiest source of getting money in the door today. You may assume, for the purposes of creating the initial forecast, that all outstanding customer balances existing today are collectible in the next 90 days, or 13 weeks, and in the spreadsheet, identify your best estimate of when such receivables will be collected. Regrettably, another common failing of companies in trouble is that receivables are allowed to lapse beyond 90 days, and in some cases cannot be collected at all. Yet managements have failed to face up to this fact, and as a result, receivables can often be significantly overstated on the balance sheet.

Your group of existing customer receivables can be summed up in a line entitled "Weekly Cash Receipts." As you will see in Chapter 2, *What's Yours is Yours*, specifically devoted to customers and cash receipts, your goal for a successful turnaround should be to have your customer collections average less than 42 days outstanding, with an additional target of completely eliminating bad debt write offs..

The next set of rows on your spreadsheet will represent a forecast of future revenues, from existing or new customers. If you have contracts with known clients, these should be identified in a separate line item, along with the expected timing of those revenues. If you do not know from whom those revenues are coming or if the individual amounts are small, but the customer base is large, you should just amalgamate those amounts into one huge amorphous blob.

These amounts should all be summed and the total called "Weekly Revenue."

Based on your historic knowledge of your actual cash collections, you should now apply an average collection period to these revenue amounts and show that total as being received in the week you have historically seen the collection. This total should be called "Weekly Expected Revenues."

When you add these three totals together, opening cash, weekly cash receipts, and weekly expected revenues, you will have as a new subtotal your cash available for this week's disbursements.

The next section of the spreadsheet comprises all expenses of the company, together with fixed asset acquisitions, and any commitments to repay principal on loans. It may make most sense to categorize these from top to bottom by the relative magnitude of their category. In most companies, this will be staff costs, followed by T+E, and then rent. In manufacturing companies, raw materials may be close to staff costs. In distribution companies, transportation may be the second highest expense.

If the company is really small, the preparer of the spreadsheet may want to see every staff member's name on the face of the spreadsheet. In a large company, or if the master spreadsheet is going to be distributed among many people, perhaps the names should appear on subsequent, and/or hidden sheets.

Two line items for which it is imperative that they show up on the face of the spreadsheet are overtime costs and benefits costs. The reasons for this are made clear in Chapter 4, *Zero Tolerance*, and Chapter 5, *Benefits*.

The total payroll costs should be placed in the week that money is withdrawn from the bank for that pay period's costs. This might be weekly, every other week, every 15 days, or monthly. However, as payroll represents such a large one-time cash withdrawal from the bank, placing the withdrawal in the correct week is imperative.

Normally below payroll costs will be T+E. For the initial forecast, it is appropriate to average out the previous 12 month's T+E expenses. Once research into the basis of historic costs, and revisions to policy have taken place, it will make sense to further subdivide these out either by category of expense, department, or in the cases of some high expense employees, by employee name. Maximizing the value of T+E expenses is explained with in Chapter 6, *Travel and Entertainment—Yes!*

Rent and any other monthly expenses should be applied in the relevant week.

Other expenses can be smoothed.

Finally, required monthly repayments of interest and principal on notes should appear as the bottom few rows of cash outflows.

The expenses can all be summed up on a line called "Weekly Cash Outflows."

The "bottom line" is therefore the sum of opening cash balance, collections from existing accounts, revenues from new accounts, less cash outflows, to give you a total of "Cash Available at End of Week." This becomes next week's opening balance, and the whole analysis begins again.

Day 2:
Complete the Cash Flow Forecast!

At this early stage in the turn-around process, a number of realizations usually occur to executives in an "ah ha" moment. The first is that an astute observer (CEO) now knows almost everything there is to know about why his company is not making money. In a typical environment, he will see that revenue collections are slow, many of his receivables are doubtful (even to him), his wage bill represents more than 70 percent of his expenses, travel is considerably more than he thought, professional fees are through the roof, and he had forgotten about how debt repayment schedules make his cash flow even more negative than the losses he is reporting. He is now probably very willing to work on reducing costs!

Fuel Consumption and Range—Comparing Actual With Forecast

As a pilot continues his flight, he is constantly comparing his actual fuel burn to the expected consumption. He needs to verify this calculation frequently because if he has met an unexpected headwind, or for some other reason his fuel consumption exceeds what he expects, he will have to land at an intermediate airport. A great example of this is an Air Transat Airbus 330 transatlantic flight in 2001 that because of a fuel leak, had to glide to a power-off landing in the Azores.

And so it is in a company, where it is imperative that at least weekly, the actual cash burn is verified against the expected cash position in order to ensure that targeted expense savings are having the desired effect and customers are paying as promised.

The New Direction

How will you fix your financial problems? Chapters 3 through 13 will focus on bringing expenses under control, but first, let's talk about getting emergency cash in the door from our cheapest and easiest source, our existing customers!

Day 3:
Collect the Cash!

CONCLUSION

The first priority in any turnaround is to control the cash. The 13-week cash flow forecast must be created during the first few days of an assignment so that a full understanding of where the money comes from and goes to can be obtained. Once these numbers have been identified, priorities for control can be set, and plans for expense reduction put in place. The cash flow forecast will also visually show how badly the company will be performing without changes, and demonstrate the positive impact of how effective changes can be.

CHAPTER 2

What's Yours Is Yours

Or How Receivables Collection and Revenue Forecasting Creates $1.5 Million of Free Money for a $50 Million Company

> *SITUATIONAL AWARENESS*
> Definition: understanding where you are in relation to objects on the ground and in the air, external environmental factors and the condition of your equipment.

When I teach students to fly, I tell them that their number one priority is to stay alive, but that only 10 percent of the skills required to keep them in the air are the motor skills they use to operate the controls of the airplane. The other 90 percent relate to *situational awareness*. In airman language, this is defined as: knowing where you are at all times in relation to objects on the ground and in the air, (i.e. distances between you and the ground and clouds, other planes, and restricted airspace); the weather you expect and what you are actually experiencing; and anything else lurking nearby ready to kill you! In addition to this compelling list, you also need to listen carefully to the engine noise so that you can understand what the plane is telling you about its own condition, and air traffic controllers telling you where they would like you to go.

Just as when you fly a plane there is a critical need to stay alive, so there is when you run a company, and situational awareness is equally important there. As CEO, you must know what is happening with your staff, vendors, customers, specific competitive threats, and the macro-economic environment. And of course, "listening to your engine" means being fully aware of your financial condition by reading and understanding the 13-week cash flow forecast. And it's possible that you have an air traffic controller telling you where to go as well, except that this person might be the banker with his loan covenants—quite a tall order to follow.

Maintaining situational awareness is critical! The key to staying alive, above all else in business, is getting cash in the door. As CEO or CFO, your job is similar to the star of the circus act whose goal is to keep as many plates spinning as possible. The plates you must keep spinning include maintaining the drive for new revenues even while being the agent of change in your company. Hence the link between receivables collection and revenue management, not only as shown on the cash flow forecast but also in your day to day active management. While collecting immediate cash can be the short term savior of the company, the company will only survive long term by making new sales.

Let's learn the secrets to solving the immediate problem, collection of outstanding receivables.

Getting Cash in the Door—Receivables Collections

A very strange paradox often reveals itself in troubled companies—if you are running out of cash, why do you still have millions of dollars of customer receivables on your books? It is a fact of life that companies in trouble often have overdue receivables double or triple the amount that well managed companies of the same size will have outstanding. The common problem is that all customers are reluctant to pay but under-performing companies let them get away with it. Why don't they want to pay? Contrary to popular belief that everyone is trying to delay payment to the maximum to keep their hands on their own cash, in most cases, our receivables problems are of our own making. And as a result, they can and need to be fixed by us as well.

The key is to find out why the customer is holding up payment. Most companies have no idea of the reason because of the artificially created barriers between sales and finance departments. Invariably a salesman is too busy focusing on his next sale to get his hands dirty with "accounting" or he feels that his relationship with the customer is "too important" to ask the customer about why they have failed to pay for the previous delivery. Or he is too concerned that he'll find there is a problem which needs to be fixed and will require more "non-commissionable" work for him. Please don't conclude that I am laying all the blame on the salesman, I'm not. Without a sale, there is no company.

Rather, the likelihood is that the salesman is only behaving like this because your current measurement and reward systems for salespeople pays commission on booked revenues instead of collected revenues.

Once a salesman's commission plans are tied to his collections, you can almost do away with credit checks, because a good salesman can smell a bad credit risk a mile away!

There is a good rule of thumb which states that once a receivable gets to be 120 days overdue, it is probably dead under the current management which has let it get that far. However, don't give up. My biggest success in bad debt management was collecting $250,000 over three years past due from a company which had been acquired twice subsequent to the original sale! Which shows that getting all the money owed to you is possible, with a little work and a little creativity.

There are usually only six generic reasons why an account receivable becomes delinquent:

- Bad product,

- Bad delivery,

- Bad invoicing,

- Bad follow up.

ALL OF WHICH ARE IN OUR CONTROL!

Two remaining reasons for non-payment which aren't in our immediate control are:

- Bad economy, and

- Bad customer.

These reasons make themselves known to us in the following 23 frequently given excuses as to why a customer has not paid what you believe is a valid invoice:

- There was no original signed PO.

- The product doesn't work as advertised.

- Delivery was to the wrong place.

- Delivery was incomplete.

- Delivery was the wrong product.

- There was no follow up service.

- There was no installation.

- There was no report of the job being completed.

- There was missing paperwork, warranties, etc.

- The invoice was not received.

- The invoice was wrong.

- The invoice went to the wrong person.

- The invoice needs multiple approval signatures.

- The invoice was lost after receipt.

- The invoice was wrongly entered into the customer's accounting system.

- The check was sent but to the wrong address.

- The check is awaiting someone's signature.

- An electronic check was sent to the wrong account.

- The customer makes creditor payments when the creditor calls and asks where its money is—this is the first time you've called.

- A new CFO has taken over and wants to review all old contracts before paying any of them.

- A new clerk has been appointed and has not yet been able to work through the pile of invoices.

- A new C-level executive has taken over from the previous approver and has not yet got around to approving your invoice.

- They are just a bad customer whose modus operandi is not to pay until threatened with legal action.

And then of course, there is always the catch all, the one which we often assume, that they have no money. Now, if that assumption is correct, we may as well close our doors today, because we will never get our money if we think our customer doesn't have it to begin with.   However, that is just one possible explanation. I have already provided you with another 23 possibilities, all of which I have encountered as I have garnered money for my clients. But how do we determine which of the 23 is actually the correct one, or ones?

Start with a phone call to the client. And who should do this? In the first place, the invoice clerk, revenue accountant, receivables manager or other financial staff, at the lowest possible level in our organization, who has input to the invoice. At this stage of the game, we are playing 20 questions—we are trying to find out why we have not been paid. We are not yet applying pressure, negotiating or otherwise seeking what is owed to us; we are simply trying to find out why the client has not yet willingly sent it to us.

By not attempting to make any collections efforts at this point, and by using our lowest level of staff, we are not perceived as threatening, and we are keeping our own negotiating positions in reserve. We may not even need to negotiate at all; we may find that the reason for non-payment is something that WE did wrong and is under our control, such as sending a defective product, or invoicing incorrectly.

Before we make our first phone call, we need to introduce the first in our new series of written controls, the client phone log. Beginning today, every phone call we make to our clients seeking money must be documented with the following information. Keeping track of such information gives us all of the power we need in follow-up calls.

- Date
- Time
- Number called
- Person spoken to
- Position
- Notes of conversation

- Agreed to follow up items by them
- Agreed to follow up items by us
- Anticipated date of next conversation

Before you make the first phone call, ensure that you have the client's payment history in front of you, along with the unpaid invoices (all of them—even those which are current). If invoices are severely late (45 days or more), you may want to make some calls internally to the salesman or others who might have had client contact to ask if they know if there is any reason why the customer may not have paid the invoice, or if there are any delicate issues which you need to be aware of.

Once you are fully prepared with background, you are ready to make the call. The phone call dialog can go along the following lines:

- Confirm that the person you have dialed is in charge of dealing with supplier invoices, specifically yours. Some large companies may divide their accounts payable responsibilities among a number of clerks. Some may deal with a certain section of the alphabet, or a certain geographic region so it is important to verify you are talking to the correct person before launching into details. If you are not talking to the correct person, ask whoever you are speaking with to put you through to the right person or provide you with that person's direct dial number so you don't have to deal with automated menus on your next call.

- Once you have the correct person on the line, confirm their name, position, and direct telephone number. Later on, you should get email and fax numbers as well.

- Then ask them if they have all of the invoices you believe you have sent them, by invoice number and amount. This is where the process of elimination begins. If they don't have them, you need to resend—email and fax are far better than by snail mail, as you can follow up within 24 hours to verify receipt and data entry.

- If they have the invoices, but they have not yet been approved, find out why not. If it is a failure on our part to meet sales or delivery commitments, then we have to go back internally and finish those commitments.

- If it is a failure of approval at the other end, we need to sweet talk our counterpart at the client into going back internally and seeking approvals. If this is the only reason for non-payment, we need to advise our own sales department that before new orders are approved by us for shipment to this client, the old orders must have been approved by them.

- Once we have satisfied ourselves and our counterpart that the invoices have been received and are correct, we can then ask when payment might be expected. We should also point out that our terms are 30 days (assuming they are, and our invoices state that). At this stage, as we are now probably for the first time actually beginning to manage our collections, we should probably allow a week for a check to be received before we make our next follow up call.

- After making a few of these calls, we will begin to get a feel for which clients can be trusted, and which ones will start giving us the run around. We also might get a feel, based on the tension in our counterpart's voice, or from lack of calls being answered, whether or not the client might actually be on the brink of failing financially, and whether we want to make a deal to settle the outstanding invoices at this stage and no longer do business with them. Remember—if we are only making a 20 percent margin on a sale, we will have to make four or more new sales to recover the losses from one client receivable which goes bad.

Now let's tie this very important work into managing our cash. For every customer call we make, we have gained new data to be able to place a forecast value of cash coming in our door on our 13-week cash flow forecast spreadsheet. As this document is a living and working document, every morning when we open the forecast, we will have a visual reference of who to call if the cash has not come in as promised.

How to Earn $1.5 Million of Free Money in a $50 Million Revenue Company

It will not take long, by our assiduously making phone calls to customers, for us to bring our average outstanding receivables down below 42 days worth of sales (Days Sales Outstanding or DSO). This number is usually less than half of the outstanding time a typically underperforming company will be reporting for its DSO.

Here is a quick calculation of the benefit to the bottom line of reducing receivables from 90 days to 42 days, for a $50 million per annum revenue company. Such a company sells $137,000 of product every day, 365 days per year. The capital tied up by these excess receivables is $137,000 (per day) multiplied by 48, the reduction in number of days sales outstanding accomplished by bringing DSO down from 90 to 42, for a total of $6.6 million of outstanding debt.

Assuming a borrowing cost of 8.5 percent, if you can even borrow, annual interest savings from reducing your debt by $6.6 million will be $561,000. Thus the immediate benefit to the bottom line, if the added collections are used to pay down debt, will be half a million dollars.

Or, looked at another way, if the company's ability to borrow is restricted, enhanced collections will reduce the amount of loans needed to be borrowed by $6.6 million. Or, $6.6 million becomes available for investment in other projects.

However, the immediate interest saved is not the only saving you will achieve. Because the chance of a debt going bad increases with every day the debt remains uncollected, a reduction in outstanding receivables of 50 percent at the very least reduces the chances of bad debt write-off by 50 percent. But in practice, by talking to the client's accounts payable division on the 31st day after invoice is sent, bad debts going forward will asymptote to zero, as your company becomes known as one which expects prompt payments from its customers.

Average bad debt write-offs in poorly managed companies are two percent of revenues. Therefore, additional annual savings of $1 million in our $50 million company will be achieved by eliminating bad debts. In my worst case client situation, the company had been writing off 10 percent of its receivables historically. This worst case situation was clearly an indication of dissatisfaction with the company's product, yet outgoing management chose to ignore the problem and make the write-offs. All this did was avoid legal action from existing clients. It did nothing to prevent the problem from recurring in the future, with new clients, because the old clients who never had their dissatisfaction resolved never provided repeat orders.

Failure to address the causes of a serious bad debt problem leads to further negative consequences within many badly managed companies—the cost of generating new business. Many management studies have determined that the cost of generating one new customer can be 20 times more expensive than keeping an existing one happy. I'm sure if the company described above had resolved its service issues sooner, it would not have needed me to step in to resolve them at the last possible moment.

One final, underappreciated advantage of aggressively controlling outstanding receivables can offer two significant internal advantages. The first is the intangible benefits from your own finance department talking to your customer's finance department. This creates a regular, second point of contact into your customer, besides your salesman to their buyer. The second benefit is that if you can teach your accounting and sales staff to put their personality differences away for long enough to have a sensible conversation, the information gleaned by the finance department might help the salesmen make additional sales into their existing customers. Or the relationship might provide a tip-off early warning of financial problems at the client company.

Summary of Total Expected Benefits for a $50 Million Revenue Company—Huge!

Profit Increase:
- Savings in interest payable on cash no longer needing to be borrowed: $500,000
- Elimination of bad debt write offs: $1 million
- TOTAL PROFIT INCREASE: $1.5 million

Capital Reduction:
- Additional capital available: $6.6 million

Intangible Benefits:
- By engaging accounting with salesmen:
  PROBABLE ADDITIONAL SALES

To demonstrate just how significant to profitability running a watertight collections department is, look again at the figures we have calculated. To obtain the same increase in profits of $1.5 million from increased sales, which is what we achieve by eliminating write-offs and bringing DSO down to 42 days in the $50 million revenue company and assuming a gross product margin of 20 percent, an increase in sales of $7.5 million would be required. In practice, it is a lot easier to bring receivables back under control than increase sales by 15 percent!

Finally, if you are the CEO of a public company, you must attest as part of your audit report that you have complied with the provisions of the Sarbanes-Oxley Act (SOX), which requires good financial control. As Accounts Receivable is often the largest or second largest asset on the balance sheet, and since the accounts receivable department interacts with almost every other department in the company, weaknesses in the financial controls of Accounts Receivable can lead to increased risks in other areas. As CEO, you therefore want to establish and maintain strong internal controls that meet SOX standards, to avoid any of the negative consequences of not doing so.

Using the 13-Week Cash Flow Model for Revenue Forecasting and Sales Management

Collections are great for getting money in the door immediately, and must be assiduously followed up at all times going forward. Once you have the customers trained, reap the benefits of that. But how do you ensure that money continues to come in the door and the company will grow?

The fact that a once profitable company is now losing money means that one situation with two possible causes has been allowed to occur. The situation is that revenues are below expenses. The causes are that either expenses have grown too large for the volume of sales, or sales have fallen too low to support the expense base—or usually, a combination of both. And in both cases, lack of controls has allowed this.

We have introduced the 13-week cash flow forecast in Chapter 1; in Chapter 3 we will define the *Organization Chart du Jour.* We have stated that these two documents are the only two documents you will need to run the company at the present time. So how do future sales revenue forecasts tie into this hypothesis and get reflected usefully on the cash flow forecast?

One way is to expand the 13-week forecast into the future and make it a full year forecast. This expands the worksheet horizontally by adding new columns for the out months. These columns do not have to be week by week for 52 weeks, because at this stage, beyond three months is impossible to predict by week. Instead, add monthly columns for the next nine months, and perhaps look out even further by introducing quarter by quarter columns for the second year.

We should also expand the 13-week forecast vertically by including the dates of known cash receipts from collections of existing accounts receivable, by named account, as well as estimated collections from projections of yet to be signed future sales.

Look at the top few lines of the cash flow forecast in Appendix 3. You will see that they fall under the heading of "revenues." In companies with a small number of large contracts, many of these lines might be filled out with names of clients. In companies with large numbers of smaller clients, perhaps the lines would represent an individual salesman's forecast or a geographic territory or a product line.

What is important for managing this data and the profitability of the company, and for converting the numbers on the spreadsheet to measurable cash in the door, is that the data on each line—whether client name, salesman name, geographic territory or product line—is measurable. And it can be designated as being the responsibility of a single individual within the organization!

Creating this level of detail on our 13-week forecast has yet another advantage in moving the turn-around forward! At a number of my clients, by the time we had reached this point and found that we were trying to document specific data for the first time, existing management had another "ah ha" moment. It had come to the realization that "no one really" was responsible for that level of detail. In many cases, accounts had just matured, or the original salesman had quit, or the client just placed orders without going through a salesman. While every salesman for sure keeps track of the commissions he is owed, often no one has responsibility for total account management. This is frequently true for accounts which are known as "house accounts." These accounts may be so designated because the original salesman who brought in the account has left, or because they belong to the VP of sales, or because they cover multiple territories.

Whatever the reason for its "orphan" status, this type of account is usually left to its own devices and fails to deliver revenue to its potential. And also, it probably has the greatest percentage of commission paid out on it because multiple sales reps will claim some input to managing it! Our 13-week cash flow forecast will change that!

The Revenue Forecast—and How It Increases Sales

Successful sales management is one of the most complex jobs in the organization, partly because of the nature of the person being managed (usually an independent spirit who doesn't like being managed) and partly because so much is riding on the efforts, the outcome of which is usually a binary decision—either you win the account or you don't. Coming in second is really rather meaningless.

Nevertheless, in order for the company to be profitable, salesmen must be productive, and ideally the compensation structure, the break-down between base and commissions, will be such that the company's and the salesman's personal interests are aligned. There are many great books and seminars on how to become the world's best salesman or sales manager, and Brian Tracy produces some of the best. *Failure Is Not An Option* does not make any attempt to improve your sales skills! Nor will it, by itself, make you the best motivator of staff, or the most welcome of visitors in your client's purchasing office. However, following the administrative suggestions described in this book will enable you to glean more revenue from the same staff and the same accounts, even without changing your personality, method of business, or hours on the job!

It has been proven that simply by keeping track of each line by line item in the revenue forecast, companies are able to improve their results and determine how successful each of their salesmen is.

To complete the revenue forecast, an example of which is shown in Appendix 3, assume that we are dealing with clients who make large individual sales—for example multi-million dollar, multi-month consulting contracts, or multi-million dollar machine tool purchases. In such a business, a salesman may be dealing with a universe of 200 potential clients at any one time, of whom maybe five are existing long term customers, and five are likely to make purchases in the next few months. My preference in terms of what the revenue forecast will look like is that each of the currently active or hoped to be active accounts will appear by name on one line each. The rest of the "to be" universe

THE DEVIL IS IN THE DETAILS

"You're on my list!"

will appear aggregated on one line using the law of large numbers to guess what gross revenues will materialize from currently unspecified clients.

Many salesmen keep their information in their head, or on Excel spreadsheets. Others will use software such as *SalesForce*. No matter in what form the raw data is kept, identifying it as a one year time line, transferring it to the master 13-week cash flow forecast and breaking it into "known" and "unknown" business creates a very visual picture of the outlook of the company.

Producing this data on a report by expected results also provides a good look into the relative performance of the members of the sales team and when drilled down into even further, can identify the true contribution of each salesman and each account to the company's profitability. It should be used to prompt questions about an account, and will immediately identify how close the salesman is to the customer. It will also enable senior management to identify where there may be internal problems with regard to product quality, delivery and administration.

In addition to being used to prompt questions, a methodology which is very effective at enhancing sales management is the product from Miller Heiman called *Strategic Selling*. The total product includes a book and worksheets. The book describes in detail how to use *Strategic Selling* to approach an account in order to make a sale, but the most important document in the methodology is a "Blue Sheet" which asks about 20 questions concerning the account. Knowing the answers to these questions means that the salesman has a thorough understanding of the account and at least in theory, is in a strong position to win the account. Not knowing the answers to more than a few questions usually indicates a salesman who is doing a poor job, and who has a low likelihood of winning such an account.

I have used Blue Sheet reviews with salesmen to identify where a sale was a lot further away than previously imagined, leading to cuts in revenue forecasts of as much as 75 percent. This was not good news, but knowing how weak the forecast was early on enabled actions to be taken to recover from the situation.

When the revenue forecast is used as a review document by the entire executive team, it can produce a window onto the trends in the business, and highlight potential problem areas throughout the company at a very early stage. These problems can include new product development, competitive issues, pricing and service, as well as the impact on the business of macro-economic trends in the outside world.

Conclusion

Collecting receivables is an immediate source of easy financing.

Managing receivables effectively and eliminating write-offs has the same contribution to profits as increasing sales by 15 percent.

Incorporating a revenue forecast into the cash flow forecast spreadsheet is an effective sales management tool and by itself leads to enhanced revenues.

CHAPTER 3

The Organization Chart du Jour— How It Can Be The Biggest Cost Saver of the Entire Turnaround Process

"You Can't Add Resources When You Are in Space!"

It was April 13, 1970, when possibly the most well known words from the Apollo Space Program were heard around the world: "Houston, we have a problem." That explosion aboard Apollo 13 ignited a frenzy of activity on the ground in a race to find a solution to keeping three men alive, a quarter of a million miles away from home, while bringing them safely back to earth. In one of the most instructive scenes in the movie *Apollo 13*, the ground support team of engineers is shown working with only the resources aboard the space craft to figure out how to find a solution to the problem of insufficient carbon dioxide scrubbing capacity. When one of the engineers suggests that perhaps it can't be done, Eugene Kranz, Flight Director, tells the team in no uncertain terms that "failure is not an option."

It is with great respect for Mr. Kranz that I chose to title this book, *Failure Is Not An Option*, after his own words, because just as in the Apollo 13 control room where everyone had to believe the astronauts were going to survive, in order to produce a successful business turn-around, the mantra of everyone who remains with the organization must also be that *failure is not an option.*

That statement raises the question of whether everyone should be on board the organization to begin with. This is an important question because in any service company, frequently 70 percent or more of re-curring expenses are direct payroll costs. And even in a manufacturing company, payroll often represents 50 percent of costs. When compensation represents such a large proportion of total outlays, it is clear that trying to cut expenses without focusing on payroll is a fool's errand. Yet I have seen many organizations attempt to cut expenses without cutting staff. For example, by banning all travel, training and marketing! All this does is emasculate those whose job it is to bring in new customers, or to improve the quality of existing employees!

I once attended a government department's "citizen's forum" seeking ideas for cutting $20 million from a $500 million budget which embraced the consensus idea of "making employees pay for their own coffee," (instead of it being provided by the government) as one way to tackle the problem! And we wonder why the real reasons for excessive government spending are never addressed!

Total Compensation is often a black hole! Where does all the money being spent on payroll go to? Who is paid what? Who reports to whom? What do they do? And most importantly, would you notice if they were gone?

The answers to most of these questions in the majority of under-performing companies is "we don't know," because, within a culture which does not control expenses, is an accompanying culture of not managing people. Either the company has become fat and happy, and no one cares, or the CEO and other executives like to be liked and won't take the hard management decisions of judging others' performance. This leads to the company becoming overstaffed, good performance not being rewarded, poor performance not being penalized, laziness becoming the order of the day, and abuses of privilege rampant.

So how do we find out who is on the payroll and what they are supposed to do? We need to create an organization chart—because if there is lack of control, you can bet your first week's consulting fee that there won't be a current chart.

The chart we will create will be known as the *"Organization Chart du Jour."* Why? Because, like the restaurant's soup du jour, we expect it to change every day until we get staffing under control. We need to know our current head count at all times and who is responsible for accomplishing what needs to be done. But until we have identified who we would like to be members of the long term team and what results they must achieve, we do not want to create a permanent organization chart.

The best way to create the organization chart is to start by obtaining a roster of employees from the human resources manager. The goal at the end of the exercise is to have created on one piece of paper (or one front sheet together with supporting documents containing other departments) a clear picture of how the people in the organization relate to one another.

The organization chart we need must contain the following information. Each employee's name should appear in a box containing his title, and line of reporting authority. To whom does he report and who reports to him? Who are his peers? What department is he in? This will enable the next missing link, a list of his goals and objectives and who reviews his performance, to be created. This, however, is a future project!

Additional information such as salary should also be identified, but probably not on the face of the organization chart as too many people might see it. Once the chart has been drawn up, we will understand the general hierarchy as it stands and can begin interviewing key managers. The purpose of these initial interviews is to make a preliminary determination of who we might want to be part of the future team, and who is likely to try to block progress. It is always illuminating to see many managers surprised (by the seeing the organization chart) who find that there are some staff reporting to them who they thought reported elsewhere, and there's also a good chance some employees will be found to be "orphans" with no official reporting lines!

Whatever we find regarding reporting lines or not, it is critical that every person in the company who is paid for their time appears by name on the organization chart. Otherwise, there will be staff that are paid, potentially for doing absolutely nothing! By the time we have worked our way down to the bottom of the organization identifying all the layers of employees, everyone on the payroll will have been placed in a box on the organization chart.

The product of this endeavor is a visual reference of who performs which critical objectives of the company's raison d'etre. In the same way that an electrical or mechanical schematic of an airplane's operating systems enable the pilot to troubleshoot and bypass a broken component within the system, our company *Organization Chart du Jour* enables us to reallocate work objectives when people leave and create a blank space on the chart.

Yes, our goal in a turnaround is to encourage people to leave. Remember, depending upon the type of company, 50 to 70 percent of the expenses are staff costs! Sometimes, mandatory redundancies are necessary, but the skilled turnaround executive can encourage the right people to leave of their own volition. The tips to staff reductions are not limited to those identified next in Chapter 4, *Bringing Staff Costs Under Control—Zero Tolerance*. All of the suggestions in *Failure Is Not An Option* regarding changing the culture for the better will lead to staff reductions. By introducing the changes described in this book, you will become one of these skilled executives.

Management by Wandering Around—Who Goes First?

Tom Peters was the man who is credited with coining the phrase "Management by Wandering Around." It is a valuable technique for identifying the pulse (or lack thereof) of a company, and for gaining impressions of who you expect will be likely to embrace change and who will resist.

A story to set the stage:

Some time ago, a bank invited me to turn around a chemicals distribution company. The company was losing about $2 million per year on $10 million of revenues when I was brought in. The owner had substantial real estate holdings, and regrettably, had not been previously advised against providing a personal guarantee for his company's bank borrowings. Now, with the company losing money and being in breach of the bank's loan covenants, the bank was about to foreclose on his lake front estate, a very unappealing prospect for the owner in the days when real estate was easy to sell!

I arrived at the company in the early afternoon and, after the usual pleasantries, was shown around the warehouse and introduced to whoever was standing around (standing around being the operative descriptor). After the president described the business to me, and related the history of the major customers, most of whom it seemed had long standing relationships with his company, we spent until 9 p.m. that evening reviewing the last three years' financial statements. I was then given a set of office keys, and looked forward to reconvening the next morning at 9 a.m.

As is always the case at the start of a turnaround assignment, time is of the essence, and this one was no different. The bank had given me four weeks to turn this ship around or they would call in the guarantee. So I was up bright and early next morning and at the shop by 0700. What surprised me, for a company which was losing a substantial sum of money because revenues were down substantially, was that the parking lot was already full, and the warehouse was buzzing with drivers and laborers. The trouble was they were all enjoying a smoke, reading the newspapers, and generally having a good time, as opposed to loading the trucks, checking inventory and getting an early start on their deliveries!

As the new kid on the block, I can always feign ignorance and ask stupid questions, so I put my time to good use getting to know the hierarchy of drivers. I asked about which routes they thought were the "best," who their "best" customers were, things they enjoyed about their jobs, the expectations management had of them, the controls they had to observe and the freedoms they enjoyed, how easy the job was, gripes and so on.

By 9 a.m. I was really enjoying myself as these guys couldn't believe how stupid and gullible I appeared to be by my asking the most basic of questions, and appearing not to notice how inefficient they were! So I went back to the office to leave a note on the owner's desk to say that I was still gathering information and would see him later.

By 11 a.m., (yes four hours into the day) the last of the delivery trucks had left the warehouse. From what I had seen the previous day, I knew most would not be back until after 4 p.m.—for an average time out on routes of just four to five hours, after you had allowed the drivers their one hour lunch break!

Free of most of the employees, I could now get down to business with the owner. My first question was to ask for the employees' time sheets. Sure enough, most of the drivers and warehousemen habitually clocked on before 0700, and most clocked off at about 1745, for a good 10 hour day of wages, two hours of which was overtime at time and a half, making for payment of 11 hours of "straight" time, or 37.5 percent more than would be earned for a "standard" eight hour day.

60

Worryingly, only about half of that total time was productive time, and I was already beginning to understand why the company was losing so much money. Questions were forming in my mind about payroll policies, employee supervision, route planning and inventory management, or lack thereof, rectification of all of which ultimately played a part in making this company profitable once more. But more than anything, the critical problem which allowed more than half the workforce to get away with working only half the time they were paid for was because of a complete lack of management and personal accountability—at all levels.

The Organization Chart du Jour

The rest of my second day was spent putting the knowledge I had gained about the staff into the *Organization Chart du Jour*. I fully expected this one to change rapidly, even more so than normal for the early stages of a turnaround, because the inefficiencies were so glaring.

The changes I envisaged would be voluntary, involuntary, usually beneficial and sometimes problematic. But by having EVERY person's name on the organization chart, and having their relationship to everyone else clearly laid out, it was easy to see with a quick glance, what would need to happen to strip out costs, rationalize functions, eliminate the dead wood, and turn the ship around.

As was expected, there was not a current organization chart. So I had to start from scratch. The easiest source document to use was the payroll register, as it should have reflected everyone who was being paid.

In some companies, the total payroll register contains more names than those who actually show up for work! Perform an audit.

Because the *Organization Chart du Jour* is one of the two most critical documents for the turnaround, and it will be used in many ways for many purposes, it is important to construct it completely and correctly right from the start.

Once you have identified who is being paid, the reporting relationships can be created. Rather than having a box for every individual describing their title, especially in a large enterprise, it may be appropriate just to have a list of names under a department head at this stage. The key is to get every name somewhere on the chart.

The next step in identifying where staff changes might need to begin is to continue wandering around, and interviewing as many people as you can, starting at the top. You want to get a sense for each individual's attitude and skills, and at this stage in the turn around, probably in that order. It is critical that everyone in top management understands the need for change and is willing to support the changes needed. Meetings with each member of management can also provide interesting perspectives on how they all interrelate!

Responsibility with Authority

One of the questions to ask of each of the staff you interview is reporting relationships, up, down and sideways. It is always interesting to discover that not everyone agrees on who reports to whom, or who has responsibility for managing each individual.

This discussion will also enable you to find those few employees that no one seems to acknowledge as reporting to them, who are perhaps getting paid to do nothing because they haven't bothered to ask who they report to. You might also identify if there are people whose names you have gleaned from the payroll and are no longer there, yet are still being paid! Yes this happens, sometimes intentionally, in which case you now have a fraud situation on your hands. More often, though, it is simply through carelessness, lack of controls and lack of procedures. Whatever the reason, there is a good chance that you will find a one percent or greater discrepancy between who is being paid, and who should be paid.

Word will begin to get out that leaks in the company's cash controls are being plugged, and attitudes among staff will begin to perceptibly change. However, the biggest change you can make in the company's culture will come with your next edict! *It is to ban overtime.* Chapter 4, *Bringing Staff Costs Under Control—Zero Tolerance*, discusses why and how to do this, and more!

How Does This Relate to the Organization Chart du Jour?

The overtime ban, and other policy changes will cause many people to voluntarily resign, as they realize things are no longer the same. As people quit, the duties they performed have to be reallocated among those who remain. They must NOT be replaced. New people cannot be brought on board. Think of yourself as if you were on Apollo 13—all you have to work with is what is currently on board. While life may be simpler with more or different resources, if you are an almost bankrupt company it is physically impossible to get them!

And there are three main reasons for not replacing staff: cash conservation, identifying what work is really necessary, and understanding that ultimately, ALL expenses of a company are related to headcount. The vast majority of people believe that everyone's work is necessary, and that if someone leaves and is not replaced, there will be "too much work" for everyone who is left. But what may be surprising, at least initially, is that in many cases, the most interesting observation after people have left under-performing companies is how little critical work was actually performed. Having to reallocate what they did among the remaining staff is a prime opportunity for finding out how much was relevant to increasing shareholder value. The reallocation of the duties of the departing person may go to:

- Staff laterally, (to a person of similar rank on the organization chart),

- The person below (if a relatively straightforward job) who may be capable of assuming more responsibility, and who sees this as a promotion, or,

- Back to the manager above who probably delegated this work some time ago!

Depending on how many people quit, it may be possible to merge or eliminate departments, combine sales territories, or discontinue unprofitable products. Whatever the outcome of the reallocation of duties, if there really is too much work to be performed by the remaining staff, then the least valuable work, or the least profitable customers and products must be identified and triaged. But under only the rarest of circumstances, for example, where a critical technical issue cannot be solved by anyone else, should a position be refilled, at least at this stage of the restructuring. Remember, we are in a cash crunch and it is better to take the unpleasant medicine at the beginning.

"Exit this way, non-performers first."

Management by Objectives—MBO

Once we have the *Organization Chart du Jour* in place, the next stage of the personnel realignment is to identify who is supposed to do what and how will the "what" be reviewed. For many white collar employees within an underperforming environment, this might be the first time they have been subject to goals, objectives and reviews since they left school.

At this stage of the restructuring, trying to encompass everything an employee does is an impossible task and overkill; this is especially true because each remaining staff member is being asked to take on more responsibility. However, it is imperative that the most basic objectives still be identified and written down.

Within the finance department, for example, a simple objective for the controller might be "to complete the books accurately and within six days of month end." You would be surprised by how many companies I have been involved with where book closing took a month or more, or in one case, there were actually no books to review.

For the Accounts Receivable Collections Clerk, an objective might be to bring Days Sales Outstanding (DSO) down to 40 days and have no bad debt write offs.

For a salesman, it means setting a quota and then working backwards to identify how many cold calls are required each day to generate sufficient interviews to create orders.

As with the implementation of the Overtime Ban, and the Drug Free Policy (Chapter 4, *Bringing Staff Costs Under Control—Zero Tolerance*), implementation of MBOs may encourage those staff who don't want to be subject to objective standards to quit, saving costly layoffs and possible legal claims, especially if those job holders to be laid off are members of some legally protected employee class.

Determining What Employees Really Do

In all of my engagements, I obtain the up-front agreement of the owner, CEO or investors that at least in the first instance, no one who quits or is relieved of their duties will be replaced, for the reasons discussed previously. They may only be replaced if it has proved to be impossible to reallocate all their tasks among remaining staff.

During one engagement, I was working at the client's site Wednesdays to Saturdays, allowing existing management to undertake their day-to-day responsibilities on Mondays and Tuesdays. On the third Monday morning of my engagement, I received a panicked phone call from the owner to tell me that as a result of the introduction of MBOs the previous week, the Controller had quit that morning. This was music to my ears because besides the fact that she had had a poisonous influence over the entire accounting department, her efforts and skills for the position were way below the minimum I felt necessary. For example, it took more than four weeks to prepare the previous month's financials, and even then, the statements were usually inaccurate.

After I had calmed down the owner, he said that he knew we had previously agreed not to replace anyone who quit, but this position was so critical that he needed to go to a temporary accounting agency immediately to get help. My response was that instead he, the owner, should take over the Controller's duties, because, until five years previously when he had bought the company, he himself had been its Controller.

His concern was, "Who is going to do my job and talk to the customers?" My advice was to just do it today to see what happened. My view was that the Controller had really spent her time doing very little, and that the amount of work required by the owner in "talking to customers" was nothing that couldn't be combined by the owner with the additional responsibilities of closing the books.

He agreed to do so provided we would discuss the situation again on Tuesday morning. On Tuesday, a very happy and relaxed owner called me and stated, "I have no idea what Barbie did all day; I completed her work in two hours!"

Suffice it to say that while I was acting as interim CEO, the owner was able to take over the serious controllership work while delegating to the Accounts Payable and Accounts Receivable Clerks the more mundane functions that the Controller had been responsible for, providing enhanced challenges and upward mobility for both these employees, and gaining considerable cost savings from no longer paying the Controller's salary.

Unpaid Time Off—Furloughs and Holidays— Combing Sick and Vacation Time—Fairness!!

Depending on how deep and urgent the financial situation you inherit, there may be a need to reduce total compensation expense without losing employees, and without reducing individuals' annual salaries. It may depend upon whether or not the company has human resources you may not want to lose under any circumstances, such as in a consulting environment where a specific industry skill set is rare, or if the business is predominantly seasonal.

The way to accomplish this is to offer or mandate a specific amount of time off without pay. That can be combined with the opportunity to use up accrued but not taken vacation. This may lead to another finding—that the company does not have accurate vacation records!

Typical times of the year when the least amount of productive work gets accomplished (in the US) include the Christmas/New Year fortnight, (a British term for two weeks), and the weeks which encompass the July 4 and Thanksgiving holidays.

Most US companies provide these specific days off as paid holidays, so adding some time off around them makes scheduling sense, especially if the company wants to keep all staff on board, but does not have 52 weeks' work for everyone. Considering office or factory shutdowns during the weeks around these major holidays provides an opportunity to reduce compensation expense by six percent or so, while providing the benefit to employees of additional vacation time. Whether or not any or all of these holiday closures become a permanent fixture of the company going forward will depend on subsequent growth in revenues, but for a company in dire financial straits, they offer a significant and immediate opportunity to save costs.

With regard to vacation and sick time, many US companies provide the same amount of sick leave as vacation time. In the private sector, a typical policy might be two weeks' vacation plus two weeks' sick leave. This segregation of time off is bad policy on both a moral and a morale basis. Very few staff are truly ill for so many days each year, but if they don't take the days off, they will probably lose them. This encourages staff to schedule a "sickie" for other purposes.

For a long term solution which benefits both employees and the company, HR should introduce a policy which combines all paid time off, sick and vacation, into one account. There is much research which demonstrates productivity enhancements with a proper work/life balance. For example, one of the benefits of vacation is to be able to de-stress and therefore be healthier. Allowing four weeks' vacation and no separately identified sick leave is generally better for all concerned. The benefits of combining vacation and sick leave into a Paid Time Off bank are multiple:

- Honest employees, ones who never miss work for illness and therefore are only able to take two weeks off, do not feel gypped with time or being underpaid by four percent (two weeks out of the year) compared with their dishonest peers who claim two weeks of sick days even when not ill.

- Everyone can plan for their time off.

- The company can use its new "generous" time off policy as a recruiting advantage for attracting the right sort of staff.

- Taking the opposite tack, and not sharing the cost savings with employees, if the company decides that its old separate policy offered too many sick days off, it might choose to reduce the total combined days in the new policy.

As an example, one of my clients looked at the usage of vacation and sick days and found that the "average" usage of sick leave was eight days per year out of ten allowed, and ten days of vacation, out of ten allowed. By introducing a Paid Time Off Bank and decreasing the total paid time off to 18 days per year, instead of the combined possible 20, there was no cost to making this change, and morale improved as the good employees were rewarded with extra time off, and those who had been abusing sick leave were no longer able to abuse the system.

Benefits of Reduced Headcount in a Turnaround Situation

Besides the fact that compensation by itself is the largest single source of expense for a company, almost every controllable overhead expense of a company is directly related to headcount, from benefits, travel and entertainment, office supplies, space, and direct management costs. So the fewer employees required to perform the functions, the lower the total costs. Introducing the *Organization Chart du Jour* and judicious use of the other examples provided above should create the opportunity to reduce payroll by 20 percent or more.

Conclusions

1. Staff costs are the largest expense of a company and consequently, must be identified.

2. The *Organization Chart du Jour* enables staff cost identification. It shows how everyone relates to everyone else and how work flows within the company.

3. Once an *Organization Chart du Jour* is in place, staff will conclude that performance is important and may well rise to the challenge. Those who don't, have self-identified themselves as weaker team members.

4. Introducing unpaid leave at holiday time can reduce payroll costs without reducing capacity.

CHAPTER 4

Bringing Staff Costs Under Control— How to Reduce Staff Significantly Without Firing Anyone!

Zero Tolerance—The Overtime Ban and the Drug Free Policy

There's an old joke in England which pokes fun at one of the professions, Chartered Accountancy. The joke is as follows: A balloonist gets blown off course by unexpected winds and lands in a field. Seeing a man walking toward him he hails, "I say my good man, could you tell me where I am?" The man responds, "You are in the southwest corner of Farmer Smith's 12-acre corn field." Perplexed, but unperturbed, the balloonist responds with another question: "Tell me my man, are you by any chance a Chartered Accountant?" With this the man smiles and says, "Yes, but how did you guess?" The balloonist responds, "It's obvious, the information you have provided me with is totally accurate but utterly useless."

I often feel that this response could describe conventional financial reports presented to management and especially to shareholders. Many hours are spent by accountants determining whether or not the numbers presented are "totally accurate" in accordance with Generally Accepted Accounting Principles (GAAP). Yet, for management purposes, GAAP accounting is useless, as I explain below. And, while compliance with the letter of US GAAP has often been used to paint financial pictures which are not in the spirit of appropriate accounting, they would not pass the specific audit requirement in the UK; that financial statements not only conform with generally accepted accounting principles, BUT ALSO present a "True and Fair View" of the business.

In 1988, F. Ross Johnson, CEO of RJR Nabisco at the time of its hostile takeover, was quoted in the book *Barbarians at the Gate* as being an accountant of great skill—he took Generally Accepted Accounting Principles to their generally accepted limits!

The most egregious example of GAAP being of no value to shareholders was during the downfall and subsequent collapse of Enron. Even Enron's financial statements were prepared in accordance with the GAAP of the time as they related to Special Purpose Entities (SPE). But if they had been subject to UK Auditing Standards, they would not have passed the requirement for a True and Fair View, because the SPE's were created specifically to distort reported financial performance.

Only after Enron's collapse, when it was observed that cash flows bore no relationship to paper profits were the rules concerning Special Purpose Entities changed. And even though the media (CNBC and commentator Larry Kudlow in particular) screamed endlessly in early 2002 that Arthur Andersen should share the blame for Enron's demise, the acquittal of Andersen by the US Supreme Court on all charges in May 2005 was given virtually no press coverage, even though the media had played a major role in causing over 80,000 innocent employees of Andersen to lose their jobs.

While the financial antics of certain executives of Nabisco and Enron are extreme examples of large companies manipulating accounting rules for their own gain, at a more typical company level, let's look at two particular situations where GAAP reporting is just as useless.

Externally, if you are a shareholder in a publicly traded company, it is impossible for you to find out what proportion of your company's total costs relate to payroll. Instead, your SEC compliant annual reports will group company expenses into such categories as "cost of goods sold" (COGS), and "selling, general and administrative" (SG&A). COGS will include all the costs associated with payroll and benefits of the workers employed in producing the goods for sale, as well as the cost of materials, energy, and depreciation of machinery. And anything else the company's cost accountant wants to absorb in such classification. But how much of that cost is actually wages, how much is overhead, and how much is material?

Within SG&A, how much is salaries, how much is travel, and how much is advertising?

SEC reports produced in accordance with GAAP don't tell you, so you are in the same position as the balloonist in the field at the introduction of this chapter. The information the company has provided you with is totally accurate but utterly useless.

Internally, within a typical manufacturing environment using "traditional" management accounting systems, Cost of Goods Sold will include not only the direct labor costs of manufacturing employees, (wages, overtime, taxes and benefits), but also apportionments of overhead staff salaries determined to be related to supporting production, and arbitrary allocations of facilities costs. A budgeted level of production will have enabled these costs to be apportioned to the quantities expected in order to arrive at a "standard unit cost of production." Production of more or of less than the budgeted quantities of goods will lead to cost "variances," either positive or negative.

Positive variances are traditionally seen as being good! Yet in terms of cost control, these standard cost measures are utterly useless.

For example, if a production manager understands standard costing, he might be incented to increase the number of units he produces in order to get a positive "labor variance" even though by doing so, he might be building product to inventory, where not only might it become obsolete, it will certainly will incur storage and insurance costs. Unless there was a demand for the extra units, the best solution might have been to produce less in a shorter time frame and shut down for a day!

The hypothesis that traditional management accounting misinforms traditional management is a subject for an entirely different book, but I introduce it here to emphasize that in order to find out what is really happening at your company in terms of staff costs, you MUST look at the general ledger, and you must look line item by line item, department by department, and possibly, even person by person.

In almost every company, excluding the capital intensive industries such as utilities, payroll is the biggest single expense. In service companies, it is typically greater than 70 percent. Even in manufacturing companies, payroll may exceed 50 percent of costs, but even when it is less than 50 percent of total costs, as an expense classification, it is probably still the largest single expense classification. So by itself, it is an expense that needs to be focused on. Yet, even though payroll, once identified, may "only" represent 50 percent of total costs of a company by itself, almost every other expense is driven by headcount. Some costs are directly variable, such as benefits, travel, and stationery, while others may vary as a step function, such as real estate required to house employees, administrative support, human resources, etc.

Because all expenses of a company are ultimately directly related to headcount, cutting payroll can have the biggest single immediate beneficial impact on a company's survival and profitability. This is not to say that headcount reductions should be arbitrary and capricious, or that all headcount reductions are good. Taken *ad extremis*, it would lead to a company of zero employees! However, the impact of headcount reductions can be positive, OR negative. Managements generally fear the negatives without understanding how the positives can outweigh them. They therefore fail to take the required actions because they fear only the negative impacts. But the measures described in this chapter will show you how to have positive impacts over and above the simple cost savings achieved by making the necessary changes. And, if you follow these measures, it is unlikely that you will incur the moniker "Chainsaw Al," a ruthless turnaround executive of the 1990s, because you will have to actually fire very few people—they will more than likely fire themselves.

Why Are We in a Mess?

Companies which are losing money after having experienced many years of profits typically have grown out of control. This sentence has two areas of emphasis—"grown" and "out of control." We have already laid the groundwork for controlling the "out of control" by creating the 13-week cash flow forecast. But it is here within payroll that we need to deal with the harsh reality of out of control staffing growth.

Typically, as a company's revenues grow, it is very easy to justify adding new staff to support the (presumed) increased work load. It is also very easy to allow overtime for additional production, shipping, and customer support requirements which are not met by improvements in productivity. While sales volumes are increasing, it is likely that the increased revenues will mask the effect of increased costs, although margin analyses (see Chapter 10, *There is no Margin for Error*) might show that profits are not increasing as much as might be expected.

However, when the company's fortunes reverse, and revenues decline, managers typically find it difficult to eliminate staff—and are often reluctant to cut back on overtime, which in many cases has become seen as an entitlement by employees.

To provide a real life example of the above generalization, let's return to the distribution company discussed in Chapter 3, *The Organization Chart du Jour*. On our second day at that client, we identified that most of the warehouse and distribution workers were being paid for two hours of overtime per day at "time and a half," earning the equivalent wage of eleven hours of straight time. And to add insult to injury, this was for about five hours of actual productive work.

Our ultimate goal in managing payroll expense is to pay workers eight hours of wages for eight hours of work. At the distribution company, getting to this point would reduce the direct wage bill by about 55 percent for this classification of employee. And if we could accomplish a full workday's effort from the staff, eight hours of productive work, we would require 37 percent fewer employees in that area as well.

To get to this point required a three-step process. When I explained it to the owner, he was skeptical, and waffled a bit about not being able to lose people because they were "family" (nepotism is to blame for many companies' performance problems). However, the imminent threat by the bank to take from him his lovely $4 million estate focused his mind and he agreed to the implementations described below.

The Overtime Ban

From what I had observed, we didn't need eight actual hours to do what was accomplished in eleven paid hours, we needed just five, so on our third day, the owner issued an edict banning all overtime. This edict had the usual effect. The immediate result was consternation in the warehouse, a few unpleasant words, me being called some choice pejoratives, and a reduction in hourly wages paid out, of about 35 percent!

Bingo! We have identified our first reduction in cash need.

As we are now managing this company in real time from two pieces of paper, the *Cash Flow Forecast* and *The Organization Chart du Jour*, it is time to make our first change to the cash flow forecast. After the next payroll, the line representing overtime can be reduced to zero along with an accompanying reduction in associated payroll taxes, (and ultimately a reduction in workers compensation expense).

At the distribution company, this revision provided us with another couple of weeks of cash reserves—valuable time in which to continue the changes needed to working practices, and to demonstrate to the bank that we were serious about a successful outcome.

Most of the affected employees were annoyed that this little game had been discovered. A few, the honest ones, were glad that they could be treated equitably because they had only "gone along with the game" to fit in. Interestingly, the edict also enabled me to identify which supervisors were going to be "part of the team" going forward, and which ones had no concern whatsoever for the profitability of the company. The majority of supervisors had also "gone along" with overtime, as it made them popular with the drivers, and for them, banning overtime was almost against their religion. Those who aggressively opposed this edict, moved closer to the day when they would hear Donald Trump's immortal words, "You're fired."

But even more valuable, and somewhat disappointing, I also gained an insight into how far the rot had seeped up into the administrative and management functions by observing that even some senior executives were openly against this edict.

However, once it was clear that the owner would not waiver on this decision, after all, he was working for "that suit the bank had sent in, so it was not his fault that these actions had to be introduced," the changes in the warehouse were immediate. Trucks began to be loaded at the start of the day and began their delivery routes promptly, returning just before 4 p.m. so as not to leave the impression that there was slack in the schedules. (That would be dealt with later!)

Rumors began that a few employees were really unhappy that their wages "had been cut 40 percent" and would be seeking jobs elsewhere—more good news for my client because these employees were not the ones we wanted to keep anyway, and remember, we were still 40 percent overstaffed for the current customer and route system, let alone what changes we would find later when we analyzed customer profitability (Chapter 10, *There is No Margin for Error*) or route efficiencies (Chapter 11, *Don't be Taken for a Ride—Transportation Costs*).

Now, how can we eliminate up to 40 percent of staff without resorting to the unpleasant behavior exemplified by "Chainsaw Al," which ultimately required him to need armed body guards 24 hours per day? Whether or not you agree with individuals' rights to "do drugs" on weekends, the answer is that on day four of the Turnaround, you announce the upcoming implementation of a zero tolerance, drug free policy for the workplace.

The Drug-Free Policy

In general, the worse the company is performing, the shorter will be the time horizon allowed by the bank or other investors to fix the problems. If losses exceed 20 percent of gross revenues, the more urgent becomes the need to trim staff costs.

As an outsider, even after wandering around for a few days, observing and interviewing key managers, you do not really know who is a good performer and who isn't. You also have not yet been able to determine who among management to trust and who will put their friends' interests ahead of the company's.

Therefore, if a major culling of staff is needed immediately, which, in most cases is the only way to get expenses aligned with revenue in the short term, there is a good chance that if you arbitrarily pick names, you will make mistakes. In addition, there is a high likelihood that, given that poor performance is the culmination of a great many management errors, (lack of control, lack of objectives, lack of policies, etc.), there will not be performance reviews to guide you as to who is a keeper under the General Electric/Jack Welch 20/70/10 evaluation of staff's performance called "Differentiation." There he calls for recognizing the top 20 percent, middle 70 percent and bottom 10 percent of staff and institutes policies for dealing with each in the way of education and training.

As a result of there being no performance reviews, any attempt at making a "scientific" ranking of staff at this stage is impossible. That will come later.

Therefore, in the absence of objective data, you only have the following common methods for reducing staff available to you:

- Last to join, first to leave;

- Arbitrarily setting across the board cuts—to be implemented by those who got you into this mess in the first place;

- Basing decisions on first impressions.

Other methods such as targeting the highest paid could potentially lead to age discrimination lawsuits (if you assume that salaries generally rise with tenure), and in any case, it is possible that the most highly paid contribute value commensurate with their compensation.

Given the lack of hard performance data, how should you choose who should leave so early in your tenure at the company? And how do you convey to the staff that it is not your sole function to fire people and therefore become feared rather than revered? If your only goal as perceived by employees is to fire people, no one will work with you and your objective of saving the company will become that much more difficult, if not impossible to achieve.

> **The easiest, cheapest, smoothest and therefore best way to reduce headcount, which also avoids any threat of litigation, is for employees to realize for themselves that they don't really want to be part of your new organization, so that they leave voluntarily.**

And the easiest way to obtain a self selecting mass exodus of the least valuable employees in a company is to introduce a "zero tolerance, drug-free policy." In one company I managed, 30 percent of the employees resigned over six weeks—which was just what we needed to break even.

This book is not the place to discuss whether or not drugs should be legalized, or whether or not a company should legislate what its employees do in their free time. It is a "how to" manual providing step-by-step instructions for you to make your company more profitable. Creating a drug free workplace is possibly the best single measure you can take.

Appendix 6 cites numerous academic studies which confirm this analysis. The following benefits accrue to a company which is drug free:

- Higher productivity and quality of output
- Greater reliability and safety
- Less absenteeism
- Fewer accidents
- Less waste

- Lower incidence of crime—petty theft and vandalism are all dramatically reduced

Your benefits—all of the above PLUS lower insurance premiums!

As simple practitioners of the art of managing, you may not be interested in what some pointy headed PhD's academic research has determined. You may even scoff at such studies, evincing the unspoken thoughts that what academic researchers in their ivory towers pontificate on is totally irrelevant in the real world. Well if that is your view, I have some interesting real world data to support this policy!

Insurance companies, whose sole function in life is to actuarially identify risk and price it such that no matter what population or peril is insured, in the long run the insurance company will take in more in premiums than they pay out in claims, also show that running a drug-free

Work is OK but...overtime is great!

workplace is safer and more productive. In implementing company-wide zero tolerance drug-free policies in manufacturing and transportation companies, combined with making convictions for DUI firing offenses for drivers (as they are for airline pilots), I have seen liability insurance premiums drop by 50 percent, workers compensation premiums drop by 10 percent and health care premiums drop by 5 percent. (Note—any references in this book to healthcare savings are likely to be subject to change as parts of the 2010 Healthcare Bill are enacted or repealed).

Implementation of the Drug-Free Policy

To be legal, a drug-free policy must be uniform in all of its manifestations. This means that no one is exempt from complying with it, being subject to testing, or being the recipient of its ramifications. It must include everyone from the President on down in its randomness for testing purposes. The policy must state, in effect, that the company's premises and property are subject to zero tolerance for controlled substances, and that any employee found on company property to have drugs in their possession— in their clothes, cars, lunch buckets, overalls, or briefcases, will be subject to instant dismissal. In addition, employees may be subject to random drug tests and if traces of controlled substances are found as a result of those tests, that will also lead to dismissal.

Given the significant impact of this policy, and the prevalence in a few states of the allowance of "medical marijuana," it is advisable to seek a third party Human Resource consulting firm or attorney to create the policy to ensure its compliance with ever changing state laws.

A memo should be drafted for all employees, describing in extreme detail, every aspect of the new policy, and in order that current drug users might be afforded adequate time to bring themselves into compliance with the change in the company's new working environment, an implementation date approximately six weeks into the future should be specified. The memo to employees should be in duplicate, addressed to each employee by name, with a line at the bottom for the employee to acknowledge that he has received a copy of the policy and that he will comply with it or face the consequences. This acknowledgement should be required to be turned in to HR within three weeks, thus allowing the company a further three weeks before implementation of the policy to track down those employees who will fail to return the forms on time!

Why would the implementation of the policy be so far into the future, you may ask? Especially if we want a drug free environment to be part of the new culture of the company. Why not start today? Well first, if we start today, we will have to do some tests to show we mean what we say, which means immediate expense. In addition, employees may say that this is a major change in policy, and there may be users who on reflection would rather change their habits than lose their jobs. By providing six weeks' notice, they have a chance to go clean.

But the most important reason is that experience has shown that the majority of drug users will prefer to find employment where their habits are not scrutinized, and over the next six weeks, there will be many employees going to HR, not with their drug forms completed, but with resignation letters. Losing 10 percent of staff this way is not uncommon, and in one company I assisted, 30 percent of the staff resigned.

As each employee notifies HR of his intention to leave, our two critical management documents are updated—a box is crossed off the organization chart, and duties for the departing employee are re-allocated. In addition, the 13-week cash flow requirements forecast is further amended for the better by reducing the line for wages.

Of all of the policy changes that I have ever implemented, this one single policy saves the most money in the shortest amount of time. When I first introduced it, I could not believe its effectiveness.

Critics have leveled accusations that instituting a drug-free policy is arbitrary and discriminating, but any decision to remove people from their jobs is arbitrary and discriminating. When I am invited into a company which is new to me, where I have no prior knowledge of staff performance, and I can only determine people's attitudes after personally interviewing them, I do not have the time to make an informed decision which would withstand any legal challenges. In addition, if the staff number in the hundreds or thousands, to make an informed decision, assessing every individual, would require an inordinate amount of time, time which would be better spent on other efficiency measures. The research referred to previously has shown that in general, drug users are less effective employees than non-drug users, and there are other benefits (described later) which occur once a drug free policy has been implemented.

But the best response I can offer to critics is that by implementing this policy, employees who leave as a result have voluntarily chosen to quit, they have not been forcibly removed. I am therefore not perceived as "Chainsaw Al," and costs in the largest expense classification are rapidly diminished.

Conclusions

Implementing an overtime ban and a drug-free policy will have a major beneficial effect on reducing headcount and payroll expense without opening up the possibility of discrimination lawsuits.

CHAPTER 5

How to Benefit from Benefits

How to Gain a 50 percent Benefit from Benefits by Elimination of the Cadillacs and Introduction of HDHPs

Note: This Chapter was written without taking into account any changes proposed by the 2010 national healthcare legislation. It is quite possible that as parts of the bill are enacted, some of the cost saving ideas presented for companies will be significantly reduced.

As a Commercial Pilot I have to see a doctor every year for a medical examination. If I was an Airline Transport Pilot, the examination would have to be undertaken every six months. I hate these exams, because if I am deemed to be medically deficient in any way, my license to fly is revoked. As long time airline pilots joke, if they are not worried enough about job security in their bankrupt airlines, they all know they are just one medical exam away from being relieved of duty.

Few other civilian jobs require peak medical condition in order to be allowed to perform, yet most employees expect doctors' visits and other healthcare to be provided by their employers, and most employers do so. Why do they do this, and how much does it cost them? The answer to the second question is usually "too much." This Chapter provides several innovative ways that benefits costs can be reduced significantly, sometimes by as much as 50 percent, without the employees losing anything of significance but requiring a change in mindset, which benefits the company and the employee in other ways too.

Historically, health and welfare benefits began to be provided to employees as a way around government imposed wage controls on employers. However, as with any entitlement program, health and other insurance benefits are now often seen by employees as a right and by employers as too controversial to change—as it is feared that any changes to benefits plans can lead to unrest in the ranks. But both employees and employers can gain financially with properly designed benefits plans. This chapter outlines the fundamental principles of a minimal cost, highly valuable benefits plan, as well as providing a short term tip which usually identifies an immediate reduction in benefits costs of two percent. For a 300 person company, performing this exercise alone will potentially save you $100,000.

Most employers, and virtually all employees, do not understand the original purpose of a workplace benefits plan because its old moniker "health insurance" is seldom used. An insurance policy in general is taken out to guard against unexpected large losses. The cost of such a policy is usually small to each of many purchasers, because it expects to make large payments to only a few customers. But a majority of today's healthcare "plans" cover just about anything, in many cases with no or low deductibles. As a result, the plan administrators expect to pay out about as much to everyone in benefits as they take in from premiums. Therefore, premiums for such low deductible policies are very high, and rapidly increasing.

For the majority of employers that are unwilling to pass on to employees these rising fees, this creates an ever increasing cost burden to them. A better solution, if handled correctly, for both employers who currently choose to absorb the cost increases, and their employees, is to raise salaries by the cost of the increase in benefits, but require the employees to pay the increased premiums. This method of compensation provides employees with sufficient cash to pay for the premium increases, but it also begins to educate them in the true cost of healthcare.

However, even though the employee is as well off financially under this scenario, employers tend to take the "easy route" because to change a benefit plan to obtain the savings necessary to pay higher wages would require them to take the time to explain to employees how a *high deductible health plan* will benefit ALL parties. And in some cases, perhaps a union or other contract makes changing even more difficult.

An interesting dichotomy in today's environment, where the entitlement mentality is more and more prevalent, clearly demonstrates how little the average employee understands about the provision of healthcare services in the United States. On the one hand, organized bands of demonstrators will be seen on street corners rallying against "socialized medicine" but, at their place of employment these same people are likely

"Believe me, Captain...you'll feel much healthier when this is over!"

to be demanding first dollar coverage on almost any health benefit provided! And the employers are equally as guilty of encouraging this mentality as their staff. Like sheep, they all follow one another in providing Cadillac health plans for their employees, with Rolls Royce maintenance costs.

The reasons why change is hard to make is because if neither party is aware of the facts about how health care benefits and costs are calculated and administered, all parties can be making the wrong decisions. This means the company can be paying far more for its benefits package than it needs to, and the employees can also be receiving less in total compensation than they might otherwise receive, if the benefits were more appropriately structured to take account of risk/reward ratios. This is a lose/lose situation.

This is one area of restructuring where it pays to have a trusted benefits consultant/provider who will work with you to minimize your costs rather than attempt to sell you a Cadillac plan which is prohibitively expensive.

Let's explain why costs are so high for the most generous plans and how they can be cut in half with a simple increase in deductible. When Health "Insurance" used to be just that, insurance against a relatively rare high risk, an inexpensive premium would cover unexpected high costs for relatively infrequent treatments such as broken limbs or hospital operations. Routine low cost services such as check-ups, prescription medication, and the odd doctor's office visit would all be paid for directly by the patient, and the costs of such visits would be budgeted for as part of one's regular cost of living—just like food and utilities.

Because the payment was made at the time and place of service, (the doctor's office), and paid for directly by the user, (the patient), doctors' fees were, by today's prices, relatively inexpensive. But this was only to be expected, as Milton Friedman explains in his book, *Free to Choose*, with his cost/efficiency matrix. This demonstrates that a product or service is delivered with the lowest cost for the greatest efficiency or value when a consumer pays with his own money for something he receives or uses himself. In this doctor/patient scenario, the patient is interested in seeing the best qualified doctor for the lowest possible price, as payment for service is coming out of the patient's own pocket.

However, as employees demanded and employers granted lower and lower deductibles for their health benefits, health insurance plans migrated from being "catastrophic" insurance policies, insuring against an unexpected expensive claim, to "health provision" plans paying for everything. As this transition became all encompassing, with every doctor's visit being covered by "insurance," the insurance company became the intermediary between the patient and the doctor by making all the payments on the patient's behalf. Thus today's patient never sees the bill, has no idea how much the visit actually costs, and if the majority of the insurance premium is paid by the employer, probably doesn't care about that either.

Thus he is blissfully unaware of the double digit annual fee inflation which arises because Friedman's cost/quality matrix has now been turned upside down. An insurance company spending other people's money for services it does not consume is 180 degrees away from the most efficient quadrant in the matrix. The insurance company has no interest in managing costs. And when individuals spend "other" people's money, most of them are no longer interested in the cost but they still want the best quality. In this case, the other people's money is from the employer contribution which is rising at a double digit annual inflation rate.

Therefore, patients are no longer concerned about costs and will instead seek out the most convenient locations, nicest facilities, best service and best reputation, without doing their own internal cost/benefit analysis because to them, it costs "nothing." They will also ask for unnecessary treatments because of the low cost to them, putting a greater demand on the provision of the service and increasing its costs to everyone.

The above is a simple explanation for why as the majority of medical payments have migrated from patient pay to insurance pay, and as deductibles have declined, medical costs have spiraled out of control leaving employers to foot the bill.

How to Control Medical Costs—
Introduction of High Deductible Health Plans

In the majority of my client engagements, adjusting for 2011 prices, I have found that a typical family medical policy, with a $200 major deductible and a $15 co-payment for doctors' visits costs $16,000 annually. This astronomical cost is charged because actuarially, the insurance companies know that with virtually no out-of-pocket costs, the patients will visit the doctor many times a year for even the smallest sniffle. A $15 co-payment is insufficient to act as a disincentive to doctor's visits rather than allowing minor ailments to clear themselves up by use of over the counter medication or simple "grandmother" wisdom. Such a plan, covering almost everything at little or no cost to the employee is known as a "Cadillac Plan."

But what is interesting in health care coverage, and proves Friedman's cost/quality matrix, is that as the deductible to be paid directly by the employee increases, for example, up to $5,000 or $6,000 per year, the actual insurance premium may decrease by an amount GREATER than the amount by which the deductible has increased. Such a plan is known a High Deductible Health Plan or HDHP, and is truly a catastrophic insurance plan. Such a policy, with a $6,000 deductible may cost "just" $8,000 per year. If you bore the total costs of your healthcare, as a self employed individual, in terms of total payments for treatment and insurance premium under an HDHP, this means that you could have a major medical problem annually, i.e. be required to pay the full $6,000 deductible, and STILL be better off under this policy than under a Cadillac Plan. ($8,000 premium plus $6,000 deductible = $14,000 total cost compared with $16,000 premium and no deductible under Cadillac Plan). If you have no illnesses during the year, under an HDHP you will be $8,000 better off.

If premium costs are shared between the employer and the employee, as is typical at most companies, a simple start to changing the mentality regarding provision of health benefits with no cost to the employee could be for the company to pay the premiums for an HDHP and provide the maximum deductible ($6,000) to the employee, still saving itself $2,000 in annual costs. How can this work in practice? Assuming the employer wants to make the change to save money, and be "employee neutral," he can set up a S125 cafeteria plan and/or a health savings account into which pre-tax dollars can be transferred. This is where a professional benefits consultant should be involved, especially as tax law is always changing. While contribution limits currently are indexed for inflation, under proposed legislation they will be drastically reduced and potentially abolished. Thus competent tax advice should always be sought before setting up such arrangements.

What makes the introduction of HDHPs so attractive is that even if the employer is loath to "take away" any benefit, both it and the employee can still save money by the introduction of Section 125 Cafeteria plans and by the employee setting up a Health Savings Account to help offset the cost of the higher deductible.

Implementation of Cafeteria Plans

Many companies pay for not only medical benefits but also vision, dental, life insurance, and disability. If employees are not expected to pay more than a token percentage of the costs of each, they will probably select each item on the menu, whether or not it is cost effective for them. So the company might be paying for vision coverage for an employee with 20/20 eyesight, someone who himself is unlikely to use the service.

By introducing a cafeteria plan, the same benefits can be offered, but the employee is provided with an annual allowance of a fixed amount which he can then use to purchase among a number of alternatives offered. Now he will only choose what he really thinks he needs, and if he can save $8,000 by going with an HDHP, and have money left over to fund his 401(k) perhaps, chances are that he and a large number of his fellow workers will opt for the HDHP.

Use of Benefits Consultants

If you consider making such significant changes to your plans, it is probably beneficial to use third party benefits consultants to manage and explain the transition, so that any emotion participants may feel, may be explained by a disinterested third party rather than a perceived adversary.

It is easier for employees to believe a benefits consultant telling them they will be better off under such arrangements, than a company executive, especially if at least in the first year, the company passes much of the savings to be achieved on to its employees, the majority of whom are likely to be risk averse and have difficulty understanding the concepts involved.

Co-employers and Broader Choice of Benefits

I have been brought in to a number of small companies—fewer than 200 employees—where a complaint from HR managers is that the company is too small to be able to offer a choice of cost effective benefits plans. Often small companies, especially if the average age is high, will have a greater than average risk profile which prevents them obtaining competitive group quotes on their own. While this is true if these companies restrict themselves to working by themselves, there are many more options today for small companies to obtain competitive benefits plans. They can do this through trade associations, and sometimes state consortia, but one area which is worth looking at is a "co-employer" or PEO (Professional Employer Organization) such as Trinet, Administaff or Paychex. While these companies are most frequently known as outsourced payroll administrators, which, if you are a small company, is often a service worth paying a fee for by itself, the biggest benefit they offer to small employers is their buying power for benefits.

Simply signing up for their services often leads to 20 to 30 percent reductions in health premiums, especially if your existing staff is on average older than 40. The older your staff's average age is, the greater the savings to be garnered by joining forces with such an organization.

Note, not everything about co-employers is peachy. While the HR benefits options and payroll tax services are clear pluses of belonging to a co-employer, there are some significant drawbacks. These include less flexibility with how you compensate your staff, especially with regard to unpaid leave, furloughs and number of hours paid per week. In addition, there is usually a requirement for funds to be withdrawn from your bank account up to a week in advance of payroll date, which for a company in dire financial straits leads to less flexibility. Also, PEOs are likely to have legal restrictions on how you terminate staff. However, for a small company seeking to become more payroll efficient, it is certainly worth performing a cost/benefit analysis to see if the potential cost savings outweigh the disadvantages.

As a rule of thumb, if you have more than 200 employees and a dedicated HR manager, there is probably not much benefit in seeking their services, but if you have fewer than 50 employees with an average age over 40, then joining a PEO is likely to provide significant immediate advantages.

Other Ways to Reduce Health Care Premiums

Once the major changes to health policies have been selected, other corporate programs will lead to further incremental savings.

The introduction of the drug-free policy as described in Chapter 4, *Zero Tolerance for Error*, should by itself lead to a reduction in premiums of five to ten percent. Combine that with a safety program, wellness program, and regular employee communication, and your savings will add up.

Unless you are using a PEO, where many plans and providers will be on offer, consolidation of plans to just one provider from which perhaps no more than four alternative plans are offered, all of which should have deductibles in excess of $2,000, will rapidly increase savings.

The $64,000 Question—A Staff Reconciliation!

At the beginning of this chapter, I hypothesized that if your company is underperforming, uses a third party benefits administrator (TPA), and you have more than 300 employees, you could probably save $100,000. For a 200 person company the same ratio works out at $64,000.

All you need to do to claim this $64,000, which is yours, is to perform an employee reconciliation, verifying that you are only paying the TPA insurance premiums for legitimate employees. Take last month's third party benefits provider invoice, and check off the names for which you are paying insurance premiums against the most recent payroll which lists every person to whom you have paid wages. For all of my clients, the average discrepancy found between these two lists has been two percent. Against them! This means that the company is paying benefits premiums for employees who are no longer on the payroll. The higher the employee turnover, the more likely this is to be a larger number.

Why does this discrepancy arise? Remember, the one constant in all underperforming companies is a fundamental lack of administrative and financial control. There is no one person likely to be responsible for verifying the benefits invoice. The person who should be approving it is the CFO. But chances are that no one reconciles the bill each month before it lands on his desk, and as he recognizes the provider as a regular supplier, he probably will not question it.

But why is the invoice wrong in the first place? When an employee is terminated, the threat of penalty of the law is focused on getting a final pay check to the employee "right there, right now." The company usually wants to ensure that electronic equipment in the possession of the employee is returned and access to company systems is shut off. Without a standard checklist of procedures to be followed one by one when an employee leaves, notifying the benefits provider to advise them to remove from coverage a now ex-employee is often overlooked.

Put down this book, walk over to HR, ask for the last benefits invoice and the last payroll, and one by one, go through the names on payroll until everyone is matched against a name on the benefits invoice. Then for all those names on the benefits invoice that don't appear on the payroll, find out why not, and call the benefits provider to delete them. It is worth asking for a refund of prior overpayments too, but this is less likely to be honored unless you can prove that you had given notice to them previously, and the billing was a mistake on their part.

Other Great Benefits

401(k) Contributions

Employees who think to the long term are better employees than those who think for the moment. Compensating in the form of 401(k) contributions encourages employees to take a long term view both in their own retirement planning, and for the company. Offering a 401(k) into which employees can make pre-tax contributions up to IRS maximums is a cost free benefit. Making nominal contributions on behalf of every employee can assist the company avoid the "top-heavy" IRS rules. Making bigger contributions which vest over a time frame of perhaps up to five years can provide a modicum of cost relief to a company as unvested employer contributions revert to the employer if an employee quits in less than five years.

Education Allowances

A well trained employee is a better employee. So here is a benefit which has so much more benefit to the employee than it costs the company—an education allowance of up to the IRS maximum—currently $5,250 per annum. Fewer than five percent of your employees will take up the offer, yet to those who do, it can seem like a huge increase in salary, and may encourage them to broaden their skills into areas they didn't realize they had an aptitude or desire for. To those who criticize this policy as leading employees to quit once they are trained, my response is, "Do you want to employ idiots?"

Conclusions

Benefits are a big recruiting draw in a competitive hiring environment, but they should be judiciously provided. While the law still allows for HDHPs, they should be aggressively used.

Almost all benefits should be provided as "options" to be selected from a cafeteria plan, with the company deciding a fixed amount to contribute per employee.

Always ensure that the benefits you are paying for relate only to employees currently on the payroll.

CHAPTER 6

Travel and Entertainment—Yes!

How to Cut Your Travel Expenses in Half by Advance Planning and Other Inside Tricks!

There is no more emotive subject among employees than the management and control of travel and entertainment expenses (T+E). Yet one of the easiest ways to increase your company's gross profit margin by two percent is to reduce T+E spending by 50 percent. (This assumes that your company spends four percent of its revenues on travel. I have seen many companies spend much more than that). This improvement is accomplished by creating a fair, reasonable and logical T+E policy and enforcing it. But no matter how detailed, and how well thought out a T+E policy is, it is worth noting that without planning, it is worth nothing.

In this financial area, just as in the others so far discussed, there is much in common with flying one's own plane across the country. From many years of experience, the aircraft manufacturers have developed their own "travel" policy to get the plane from point A to point B in the most efficient manner. It's called the "Pilot's Operating Handbook." In it, you will find instructions on how to start the engine, how to take off, how to adjust the engine to operate most efficiently in flight, and how to land. Likewise, the FAA has its own "travel" policy. It requires pilots to have maps for the route, check the weather, identify hazards along the way, and put enough fuel on board for the journey.

But what is missing from all of these policies? The same thing that is missing from most companies' T+E policies, there is no requirement to plan ahead. Sure, once the pilot takes off, we assume he has a destination in mind, but if he only decided this morning that he was going to make the trip, and if he has planned his route of flight by simply pushing the button on his Global Positioning System to "Go Direct" he won't know if the weather is optimal, requiring diversions for head winds, whether he will have to climb significantly over mountains rather than fly around them, where he will be making fuel stops, and whether in fact there will be hangar space at his destination.

If, on the other hand, he had planned his trip some time in advance, he would have obtained fuel prices at airports en route, enabling a stop at the cheapest convenient source; he would have been able to calculate the different flying times for flying high but straight over mountains versus more miles of a circuitous route at a lower altitude; he would have identified the altitudes and locations of varying amounts of head or tailwind; and he would have been able to reserve hangar space at his destination.

And so it is with our traveling executives. In the famous words of Rowan Atkinson, the British comedian, "Do we know where we are going, how will we know when we have got to where we are going, but most important, have we got a map?"

In a typical business, where the urge is always to "serve the customer," the tendency is to do everything you can for the convenience of the customer. If that means that the customer asks you to come out and visit tomorrow, chances are you will agree, without consideration of the cost. But if a round trip air fare to see said customer tomorrow is

$2,000, but for the same time next week is $200, why wouldn't you suggest to the customer that you see him next week? In the most basic of financial terms, is the added value of seeing the customer tomorrow compared with meeting at the same time next week worth $1,800 to your company (the additional cost you will incur by seeing him tomorrow)? If your gross profit margin is 20 percent, it means you have to sell an additional $9,000 of product to recoup the additional cost of this unplanned travel.

Salesmen will often argue that "if we don't go now we won't get to see the customer," but I have never, in over 20 years of reviewing sales reports and expenses, seen a situation where a sale was obtained at such short notice. Consider the circumstances. The most usual scenario for a customer to say, "See me tomorrow," is because there is a deadline at the customer for a decision which we were not part of, and as a result, we are the last competitor in a bid. It is far more likely that other companies with long standing relationships to the customer have been invited to tender long before you hear, "See me tomorrow." The probable reason therefore for us to be asked to present is to provide a possible low bid which an existing supplier will then be asked to match.

Also consider this: if you have today been asked to present tomorrow, how thoroughly can you prepare in terms of identifying customer needs and your proposed solutions? And how relevant can the customer's research on you be? If you have a week before your trip, you can, through multiple phone calls, Internet searches and enquiries within the industry, obtain a very good understanding of your customer's needs, craft a perfect solution and even perhaps identify some reference accounts which the customer will know.

So I say emphatically—if a trip can't be planned at least a week in advance, don't make it.

Now review this Chapter's title, "Travel and Entertainment—YES!" I mean it. Travel is valuable and should continue. In fact, I would argue that probably the same amount of travel should be undertaken, but undertaken wisely. Properly planned travel and responsible use of expenses will enable the same amount of travel to be undertaken at 50 percent of the cost of current travel and, in what follows, I'll show you examples of how to implement a successful plan.

Too many senior managers are faced with travel and entertainment expenses which are out of control. They believe if they say "stop all travel," they've solved the problem—they've taken action. This edict is totally useless and will kill morale, and the company. What do these managers expect people who have previously traveled, to do with all this enforced desk-bound time—people such as salesmen trying to win new customers, CFOs making presentations to investors and CEOs attempting to find new strategic partners? If a customer cannot buy your product over the phone, you will not be able to sell over the phone. You have to meet face to face.

Your goal, as part of the 12-step plan to maximize corporate profitability, is to travel the same amount, but for half the cost. Yes, HALF the cost!

This goal IS attainable. I have attained it in every one of the turn-arounds I have managed. The implementation of smart travel is critical to the success of the entire company. Because not only does it rein in T+E spending, its enforcement sends a strong message to every employee that ALL spending is subject to review, and staff must be able and willing to justify any expense if asked.

The keys to success here are threefold:

1. You must have a clear policy.

2. It must be enforced from the top down.

3. Every employee must plan ahead. Failure to plan means you are planning to fail.

Clear T+E Policy

I have seen companies where T+E polices have stretched to 50 pages trying to provide examples of every conceivable situation that employees might find themselves in, such as how much to charge if their plane is cancelled and they have to remain in a city overnight. Such a policy is indicative of an environment where employees are perceived to either lack the common sense to deal with such a situation as if they were spending their own money, or management doesn't trust employees to act with common sense. In such a scenario, either employees or management may need to be changed!

The T+E policy should be logical. In theory, every expense which the employee has to pay on a trip which is an expense he otherwise would not bear if he were not making the trip on behalf of the company, should be reimbursable by the company. However, reimbursement

"Humm...can't wait til the last minute."

becomes abuse if an employee, while carrying out his duties on behalf of the company incurs an expense which if he were making the same trip for personal reasons he would not incur. Typical examples of this include:

- Purchasing the most expensive airline ticket rather than picking travel time to minimize cost.

- Using a limo to get to the airport.

- If self-driving to the airport, parking in the covered, close-in garage rather than the remote surface lot.

- Spending lavishly on food and drink at the airport and on the plane.

- Staying at a hotel significantly more expensive than usual.

- Using valet parking to save a couple of minutes walk.

- Dining alone at the best steak house in town.

- Renting in-room movies.

The Solution

The best T+E policy starts with the implicit assumption that travel is necessary, and that even though air travel these days is onerous, it should be relatively pleasant, safe and convenient. However, it should also be as cost effective as possible in order to safeguard the profitability of the company and the security of employment for all staff.

The overriding goal of the T+E policy must be:

"Business requiring travel should be conducted in the most cost-effective manner."

This means first and foremost that all out of town meetings be planned sufficiently far in advance that advantage can be taken of advance purchase discounts on airfares, and that multiple sales calls can be made in the same city on one trip, rather than making multiple trips over successive weeks to the same city.

> *"It is understood that meeting schedules often change, but our company policy is that WE do not change meetings, once on the calendar."*

Therefore, we would expect the same courtesy from the people we meet. We must communicate this to our meeting partners and request that they understand that we will be incurring expenses in advance of our meetings and that cancellation will cost us money. While we cannot prevent them from cancelling meetings, what we can do is limit the amount of rescheduling we do to accommodate a client, as this "early" behavior is indicative of the way they will treat the relationship going forward.

Below is the *"Three Step Plan"* method of reducing T+E by 50 percent without reduction of numbers of trips. These three areas of expense together usually represent about 80 percent of all T+E expense:

Step 1: Air

All travel must be purchased at least one week in advance, unless there are special sales which match advance purchase rates. All tickets purchased must be non-refundable, flight-specific tickets.

As an example of the savings which can be generated by applying these rules, as I write this chapter, I am taking a flight on a major airline, not a low-cost carrier, from Denver to Chicago tomorrow for which I paid $79 two weeks ago. The same flight-specific ticket for tomorrow is now $283—i.e 3.5 times as expensive, and a fully flexible ticket is $1087—14 times as expensive.

I expect to be able to upgrade to first class using my electronic stickers—which I can purchase for $60 for this segment, making my first class ticket $139. This compares with a full purchase price for a first class ticket of $1402, 10 times what I will have paid by advance planning.

In percentage saving terms, by planning and purchasing in advance, I have saved between 72 percent and 93 percent of the cost of purchasing a ticket the day before travel.

Other tricks of the trade in reducing airline expenses include the following:

Nearby Cities

Airlines love to be the monopoly supplier from a hub into a small town, especially if there are mountains in the way. Using these criteria, they can price away to their heart's content, to the extent that one route I am intimately familiar with, Denver to Durango, Colorado, 200 straight line miles, used to be priced by the monopoly provider such that a walk-up fare of $800 for a one way trip exceeded the advance purchase fare from Denver to Paris, 5,000 miles away. Today, fortunately for the residents of Durango, a low-cost carrier has entered the route and round trip advance purchase tickets can often be found for as little as $100!

While Denver—Durango is the perfect city pair for premium pricing, because of its remoteness and mountains, other larger conurbations have pricing anomalies that can be avoided by flying to alternative cities where there is low-cost competition. For example, travel to Milwaukee is often priced at three to four times fares to Chicago yet downtown Milwaukee is only 75 miles from Chicago's O'Hare Airport. Manchester, New Hampshire is just 50 miles from Boston's Logan Airport. The question has to be asked when traveling to these "nearby" cities: Is the increased cost of flying a little bit closer to your ultimate destination, compared with driving a rental car a few miles further, worth the time saving? What is the opportunity cost? Rarely is it worth more than about $50! So fly to the cheaper city and rent a car for the extra 50 miles.

Days of the Week to Travel

Do you really need to travel on Monday? Cheapest days of the week on which to travel are, in ascending order of cost, Tuesday, Wednesday and Thursday. In addition to saving money, there is a far greater chance that by traveling on less busy days, you will have an empty seat next to you, or be able to upgrade to extra leg room or first class. That by itself should be incentive enough! In addition, Saturday morning flights are usually less full, and the savings compared to a Friday evening flight are often sufficient to pay for an extra night in a hotel, providing you with an opportunity to see a cultural event in a different city.

Day of the Week to Purchase Ticket

Yes, it makes a difference on which day of the week you purchase a ticket! Data supporting this conclusion was provided in great detail in the Wall Street Journal on January 27, 2011. Airline pricing changes by the second. Not only do advertised prices change, some yield management systems are so sophisticated that they adjust pricing based on nothing more than enquiries. Try it for yourself! If you enquire about the same flight more than twice on *EasyJet's* website, the third time you enquire, the price will have gone up!

The highest prices quoted for travel are always posted on Sunday evenings, after people have spent the weekend aligning their travel plans, and on Mondays, when they are in their offices executing those plans. Don't join them! Lowest quoted prices appear on Tuesdays or Wednesdays, when airlines have had a chance to assimilate the Monday bookings into their future load factors. A number of airlines introduce special weekend fares on Tuesdays which provide you with a floor for the price for a particular route.

In general, a simple rule of thumb is to always make your travel bookings on a Tuesday or Wednesday!

Multiple City Itineraries

It used to be that one-way tickets were more expensive than round-trip, and on some airlines, that is still the case. However, most airlines allow one way ticket segments at half the price of round-trips. So if your travel itinerary is for more than one city, always price it out by the segment—it may be far cheaper than a multi-city ticket. In addition, consider using more than one airline for the itinerary. Flying onto one city and back from another is called an "open jaw." A strategy that often makes sense is to have one airline for the open jaw and a second airline for the intermediate segment. This is a necessity in many "hub and spoke" situations where a "segment" on one direct airline may require two segments via another carrier's hub and spoke.

Another advantage of buying one way segment tickets instead of round trips is that if, for some reason, you have to change your original outbound flight, but do not intend to change your return, you only have to pay a higher fare on a partial ticket. I have used this strategy many times when I know I will be traveling to a city on a certain date but am not sure for how long I will be staying. In that case, I'll buy the $79 one way for the outbound, and nearer the time buy the return ticket. I'm still saving my 72 to 93 percent on half the ticket!

Travel to Europe from the USA

It has been thirty or more years since the cities on the east coast of the USA were the "only" places from which to travel to Europe, and frequent international travelers know this. But on the other side of the pond, the same diversification of flights to the US has taken place. If you are traveling to the UK, no longer is London your only air access point. Manchester, Birmingham, Bristol, Glasgow, and Edinburgh all are served by non-stop flights from the US, as well as by long haul routes from the Middle East, Asia and Australia. There are frequently significant fare differences between these cities, yet they may only be three hours drive time apart. And the biggest advantage of all that you gain by flying into a UK regional airport compared with flying into London Heathrow (LHR) is *time*. The time it will take you from when your plane begins its descent to the time you pick up your rental car can be three hours less at the provincial airports than at LHR.

Let's consider how time adds up on a flight into Heathrow vs. any of the other provincial airports:

1. Great circle route from US to LHR is usually 20 minutes more than any of the other airports.

2. Stacking (holding) over LHR because of congestion (non-existent at other airports) can add another 30 to 45 minutes.

3. Aircraft taxiing and waiting for a gate to become available can add 30 minutes more.

4. Walk to customs and immigration takes 10 to 20 minutes more because of the mile-long terminals at LHR.

5. Customs control is usually backed up more than an hour most times at LHR, compared with 15 minutes or less at regional airports.

So as you can see, you should estimate being in your rental car approximately 3 hours after your scheduled arrival time at LHR. At one of the provincial airports, my record time from wheels touching down to getting in my car was 20 minutes!

But wait there's more (as they say in the infomercials).

Using an Intermediate City in Europe to get Half Price Business Class

Because of the multiplicity of airline routes from the US to Europe, especially to regional cities, it can often be cheaper to fly to a regional city within Europe, and then transfer to an intra-European flight to your ultimate destination, rather than travel non-stop to a major European city direct from the US. The fare discrepancies are most marked in Business Class. As an example, it frequently costs $10,000 round trip in business class from Denver to Paris with a stop in Dallas or Chicago. However, flying to Manchester (UK) from Denver in business class can often be had for $3,000 round trip, and from Manchester, there is a choice of airlines offering $100 flights to Paris! Sure it adds about three hours to the journey time, but is that time worth $1,000 per hour, the amount you will save in air fares via intermediate cities?

Travel within Europe

US travel agents with their CRS systems, and US airlines with their worldwide alliances would like to keep all of your intra-European flying on their airline partners. But within Europe, there has been a "Low Cost Carrier" (LCC) revolution in the last 10 years. From the UK, *Flybe* and *EasyJet* are two reliable carriers. In fact, *EasyJet* is now the largest European airline with hubs throughout continental Europe as well as the UK. Tickets can only be purchased on line on their own website, but at $25 for you and another $25 for your suitcase, do you really need to travel business class on a legacy carrier for a 20 minute flight? And talking about distance, as virtually no major European city is more than 1000 miles from another major city; do you really need to fly? How about taking a super fast train? In most cases, for journeys of less than 500 miles, assuming no oversea section, the train is faster, and certainly more comfortable for journeys from city center to city center than schlepping out to the airport two hours ahead of departure time to be body scanned and treated as though you were a terrorist!

Some of the best trains in Europe are Richard Branson's Virgin trains in the UK which travel at 125 mph, and the TGV in France which reaches almost 200 mph. Tickets can be purchased on line at *virgintrains.com* and *raileurope.com*. As with airfares, the earlier you plan, the better the deal. For example, on Virgin trains, a three-month advance purchase, first class single from Manchester to London can be had on a Saturday for £26, compared with a walk-up fare of £194, an 88 percent saving! In US dollars that's $40 to $310.

But there's still more!

Hotels

Using for explanatory purposes, the trip to Chicago I alluded to earlier, I would like to stay at a hotel in the Hilton chain. Looking on the web site, I find there are eight Hilton brand hotels within 15 miles of the city center, at rates ranging from $109 to $279. Given that I am going to need to travel between the airport, my client, and a hotel at some point in a day, no matter where I stay, does my hotel have to be the closest one to my client, or should I save $170 by staying 12 miles away? What are the time savings between staying at each one and how much is that time saving worth? If there is no specific reason, other than convenience, for staying closest to the client, we can save 61 percent by choosing the least expensive option within this brand.

Note—for real misers, we could have included Hampton Inn and brought the rate down to $89, a 69 percent reduction from the most expensive. And then, if we had an AAA card, we could glean a further 10 percent discount, getting us down to $80!

Car Rental

Thirty years of traveling has taught me to restrict my car rental choices to three agencies, Hertz, Avis and Alamo/National, because in general, they are all approximately equal in terms of quality of car, service and convenience, and they usually share similar locations either in the same parking garages, or on the same street if off-airport in major cities. I do not expect my travelers to have to go to miles away to the "rent-a-wreck" type operations. So for each trip, I simply check the rates of the three agencies and select the cheapest.

In my example Chicago trip, all agencies are offering a Chevy Impala as a full size choice for between $80 and $120, with Alamo being the cheapest, Hertz the most expensive. So in this case, I will choose Alamo over Hertz for a 33 percent saving.

There is never any one agency which is consistently the cheapest. All car rental pricing is done on a yield management basis similar to airlines and it is quite possible that one agency may be out of a particular car at a particular time while another has a surplus, and will be offering reduced rates.

It is worthwhile joining Hertz #1 Gold, Avis Wizard or Emerald Isle for special deals and the ability to avoid the rental counter, saving significant time on arrival.

Can you take all of the above ideas and formalize them into a T+E policy? Absolutely. Here's how.

Overall Objectives for Minimizing Corporate Travel Costs

All travel for company purposes must be planned in advance with the most economical providers used, commensurate with comfort, convenience and safety. The return on investment to the company of each trip must be borne in mind when making decisions about how to conduct the trip. Examples of what is expected in terms of minimizing costs in different areas of travel are provided in the following paragraphs:

Air

Choice of airline is a very personal affair, and most people have a loyalty to a particular airline. Employees have a free choice of airline, provided that loyalty for the purposes of generating points does not cost the company more than an independent decision would cost. However, low cost carriers such as Frontier, Jet Blue and Southwest serve many markets and typically have the lowest fares. Legacy carriers usually meet these fares when they have flights at similar times. The fares offered by these low-cost carriers will be the benchmarks against which actual fares paid are reviewed. If your selection of fare is significantly greater than that offered by an LCC, your reimbursement may be questioned.

Hotel

Safety and comfort in a quiet room are our prime concerns. Ostentation is not appropriate. In today's environment, clients would rather we spend our money wisely rather than wildly. You should select hotels which offer free Internet. Hampton, Hilton Garden Inn and Sheraton all provide good value. If you will be using a rental car, you should endeavor to find a hotel which offers free parking.

Rental Car

The company has complimentary Hertz Gold, Alamo Emerald Isle and Avis Wizard memberships for employees so that pick-up and drop-off is quick and easy. The company will NOT reimburse for add-ons such as insurance (covered by the company's liability policy), "never lost" (you should print out a map from Google; most smart phones have a GPS app already loaded on it), or fuel refill option. These options can often double or triple the cost of a rental, for very little benefit. You are expected to refill the car yourself prior to its return.

Meals

Business entertaining is important and expected. The quality and value of the restaurant should match the expected benefit from the meeting. Expensive bottles of wine are inappropriate and may be perceived as a negative by a prospective buyer who knows that such extravagance will be built into the cost of the product he might be buying.

Airport Transportation and Parking

You will be reimbursed for one round trip to the airport per business trip, calculated as the number of miles round trip from our office to the airport at the IRS allowed rate (currently 50 cents per mile), plus the number of nights parking at the economy lot rate. You may choose any means of transport to the airport, but your reimbursement will always be at the above rate.

Administration of T+E Policy

All T+E reports are to be submitted to the CFO for the periods ended the 15th and 31st of the month, within one week of the cut-off date, approved by your direct supervisor.

Note how brief and simple this policy is. Compliance is straightforward. The company conducts its business and the employee is treated fairly. The final step in the T+E policy, and the most important part of *The 12-Step Plan* is CFO review.

Without Teeth, a T+E Policy Is Worthless. The CFO Provides the Teeth

In one company I was involved with, we had more than 400 travelers each week. When I told the CEO that I expected to see all the T+E forms, he thought I was nuts. "You won't have time to go through all those forms," he told me. What he failed to realize was that I had no intention of looking at 400 forms, each with 10 or more receipts. What I was looking for was egregious travel—$2,000 charged for a two-day trip for example. Once these travelers were identified, contacted, and advised that they would not be receiving full reimbursement, word got around that "*the CFO checks all T+E.*" It did not take many such incidents for virtually complete compliance with the policy, and a 50 percent reduction in expenses, which in that particular company had been running at $4 million per annum!

The value of CFO review pays dividends in many ways:

- Employees know that there will be a second pair of eyes reviewing the expenses.

- The CFO obtains an intimate knowledge of who is putting the company's interests first—data which can be used in promotion or downsizing decisions or as part of future HR performance reviews.

- The CFO gets an unparalleled insight into how business is being conducted in the field, and is on top of expense trends.

- The value of spend by vendor can be determined and used in negotiating volume rebates or airline or car club memberships.

Simple, Catch-All, T+E Policy Thanks to Britain's Members of Parliament

In the summer of 2009, voters in Britain were "shocked" to find that their Members of Parliament (MPs) had been abusing their parliamentary expense privileges to fatten their own wallets. The British broadsheet (quality) newspaper, *The Daily Telegraph*, ran an exposé of the strange and sometimes extravagant expenses that a large number of British MPs were charging as part of their "allowances." Once the newspaper started digging, they found that the majority of MPs, in all parties, were on the fiddle. Some of the infractions were minor, but a great many proved to be very embarrassing, and a number of MPs stood down at the subsequent General Election, knowing that the voters would not approve of their profligacy with taxpayers' money.

Under the British Parliamentary system, an elected Member of Parliament, sitting in the House of Commons, represents a constituency (district), where usually he will spend his weekend, and has to attend Parliament in London during the week. As a result, unless his constituency is within commuting distance of London, he needs two houses. Recognizing this, and in an effort to diversify the membership of the House of Commons from the traditional "rich" who can afford two houses, the MP's Expense policy allowed for, *inter alia*, charging mortgage interest on second homes, cleaning, maintenance, and other incidental expenses. As is often the case when policies are not enforced, expense claims became more and more extravagant.

Under a Freedom of Information request, which was delayed and delayed, *The Daily Telegraph* finally managed to review the claims and in addition to finding that some MPs had claimed for non-existent mortgages, they found that one had claimed to have the moat to his castle cleaned, and another had claimed to have his duck house painted. For many weeks these claims became the staple of late night TV comedians, and a number of MPs chose to resign or at least not run for re-election. The scandal was so pervasive that the details were combined in a book *No Expenses Spared* which for a few weeks was a best seller.

To say the least, the revelations were very embarrassing for a very large number of MPs. Many claimed "confusion" over the policy, while others saw everyone else doing it and thought they should jump on the gravy train. But whatever the reason, the fact that publicity provided embarrassment gave me an idea to devise a simple three sentence T+E policy which could apply to everyone in every company, and if it had been followed by the MPs in Westminster, would have not caused any embarrassment at all.

The "New Simplified Corporate Travel and Entertainment Policy" is:

1. Staff are allowed to charge any reasonable expense incurred in performance of their duties on behalf of the company.

2. All expenses will be documented on a monthly expense report to which receipts will be attached.

3. All T+E Reports become open documents of the company, which means that any employee can review any T+E report of any other employee.

This is really no different from the advice your mother gave you not to do anything you wouldn't want to see on the front page of the *Wall Street Journal.*

Why is this simple policy such a breakthrough in corporate T+E management? Because instead of going into page after page stating what may and may not be claimed, what is and is not a legitimate expense, and basically treating adult employees as though they were pre-teen children, a T+E policy, modeled after the simple one above expects responsible behavior, and the control is peer review.

Implementing such a policy would treat employees as adults. It would allow them to make judgments as to how to wisely spend the company's resources. It would force claimants to really consider how they might justify their purchase of an expensive airline ticket or bottle of wine to an employee whose overtime has just been cut, or whose best buddy has just been laid off.

In practice, while a simple policy such as the one above might be attractive, a very general policy encapsulating just the three points above does not provide enough guidance for the average employee. Therefore a more detailed set of guidelines should be set and while the above policy probably sounds fine in the abstract, as is often the case, the most logical solution probably lies somewhere between the extremes. In the case of a T+E policy, the overriding goals should be as follows:

The policy should be flexible enough to allow an employee to make his own decisions, but should have sufficient oversight that abuses are caught early and not allowed to continue.

Conclusion

Put in place a policy which requires, above all, advance planning for all travel decisions, provides ideas for working travel providers' pricing systems to the best advantage of your company, expects travelers to behave responsibly, but monitors the results.

CHAPTER 7

Flying Under the Radar Screen

Easy Expenses, Professional Fees and Risk Management

Operating a private plane is often uncharitably characterized as being expensive, especially by those who perhaps would like to make populist political capital out of a small segment of society. But the benefits to companies, in terms of time saved to go to places too small to support commercial airline service, such as rural communities, and freedom to choose one's own schedule can make personal flying an extremely cost effective and competitive business tool. General Aviation (GA) as a whole also significantly enhances the economic vibrancy of those rural communities which depend on such air links for even such mundane day to day activities as UPS and FedEx parcel deliveries!

However, there is no denying that there are expenses involved with maintaining a plane. And unlike in the case of other corporate assets such as plant and machinery, where in hard times you may be tempted to wait until something breaks to fix it, for a plane, the FAA mandates time in service and elapsed time maintenance. This means that at the very least, every year your plane must be inspected and if necessary be repaired in order to maintain its certificate of airworthiness.

Such maintenance costs cannot be avoided, so the question for a pilot becomes: Are there any easy ways you might reduce your costs of plane ownership? Because your life depends on everything mechanical running perfectly, the answer is, apart from cleaning your own windows, probably not! You want a certified mechanic to do everything. But what about the situation in the company you are managing? Are there any easy expenses you can find to reduce without affecting the smooth running of the company? Here the answer is decidedly yes!

Professional Fees

Typically, underperforming companies either don't keep track of their professional fees, or they are so lacking in control that professional fees are much higher than they would need to be if the administration of a company was being performed efficiently.

Fees which frequently offer an opportunity for significant reduction are:

- Audit

- Tax Preparation and Advice

- Legal

- Marketing

- Insurance and Risk Management

Each of these will be addressed separately.

Audit Fees
Audit fees are often higher than they might otherwise be for a number of reasons. Most common is the simple fact that the audit may not have been put out to bid for some time and the audit firm has simply continued to raise their fees without any pushback from the client!

Additionally, there is always the possibility that if the client's financial situation is declining, especially if it is so dire as to warrant a "going concern" audit opinion, that the audit firm may have added a "risk premium" to their billing.

Perhaps the fee is high because additional work has been required to be performed by the audit firm, work which might have been done in-house previously by qualified staff who are no longer employed. Perhaps the client staff have become less professional in their relationship with the auditors and are producing sloppy or incorrect schedules for the auditor to review.

The best way to identify if the audit fees are higher than they might otherwise be, is to meet with the existing audit partner for his evaluation of where excess costs may have been incurred. Assuming the relationship has been profitable for his firm heretofore, he will be willing to hold this meeting—he knows that he will probably want to maintain the relationship if a "new broom is sweeping clean" and knows that it is easier to keep an existing client than find a new one.

There is a high probability that he will be able to identify ways that you can perform more and better work internally. If this can be completed in-house by a junior accountant earning $30 per hour, there is huge benefit to your company of assigning such work internally instead of paying an accounting firm's junior professional rate of $200 per hour. Another benefit of holding this discussion with the audit partner will be that by knowing the basis of the current fee structure, if it is felt that a third party bid should be sought, the basis for current fees is at least understood.

A typical saving of the order of 20 percent of audit fees should be obtainable at the conclusion of this project.

Tax Preparation Fees

If the company is losing money, the company needs the most efficient tax compliance report possible. There is no immediate value in expensive "tax planning" strategies when losses are being incurred! In addition, as tax laws change frequently, even year-to-year, any forward looking strategy based on current laws holding for two or three more years is likely to ultimately be irrelevant.

Also, take advantage of the automatic extension of time to file a tax return—September 15 in the US. Why join the millions of filers who try to file by March 15? There are no penalties for requesting an extension. Take your time, do it right, and pay your professionals at the non-peak rate!

Legal Fees

Attorneys love clients who are worried about being sued, and will give their right arms for clients whose management is indifferent to the cost of legal advice.

But if your company is seriously underperforming, to the extent that failure might be an option, you really shouldn't care about being sued. What are they going to take from you if they win anyway (you do have your D+O policy paid up, don't you?).

Frivolous lawsuits are common and usually groundless. Stand up and defend yourself against them, and make it known that the company is no longer an easy mark. The first policy change to effect is that the company will defend any and all attempts at extortion, and will treat frivolous lawsuits as such. The company's executives must agree that they will say "boo" to the goose and will obfuscate any and all attempts by outsiders to file groundless suits. Once this becomes known outside the company, the number of attempted lawsuits will decline.

Personnel Lawsuits

Attempts to sue based on the Human Resource Department's alleged discrimination are easy to file, and therefore common. In particular, especially as the poor economy reduces the number of professional opportunities, there are some unscrupulous attorneys advertising that they can extract sums for alleged sex, age or race discrimination. In most cases, the "settlement" offered up by the attorney to the corporate victim is a *de-minimis* amount—perhaps only $5,000 to $10,000. This is calculated to be an amount that a CFO might approve just so he is not bothered with defending the claim, especially if he knows the company's attorney will bill that amount just for the initial review of the case!

However, if the case is groundless, you MUST defend it in order to set a precedent and send a message outside the company that you are not an easy mark. One of my clients was once harassed by a billboard attorney who "represented" a job candidate in a "protected class" who was not offered a position. The attorney's claim of discrimination was easily shot down when he was advised that the only class of person my client did NOT have in the relevant department were Caucasian males under 40!

If you are in the right, there is no need to involve lawyers in responding to an initial threat. And in many cases, a strong response from company management without the use of lawyers is all that it takes for a threat to go away.

Business Transactions

A big drain of legal expense incurred by American companies is in the field of Mergers and Acquisitions (M+A). Many times I have been involved in discussions about whether or not a merger makes sense, and sitting somewhere around the table will be an attorney, usually listening, taking notes, and sometimes telling everyone that an out-of-the-box idea cannot be entertained. However, the company could save significant sums if it took the UK approach to initial M+A discussions. This usually involves the company executives alone determining whether an alliance makes sense, and once it has been so decided, only at that point are the attorneys brought in to draft the "Heads of Agreement" which puts in legalese what the executives are trying to accomplish.

There is really no advantage to involve lawyers in initial discussion of simple business contracts until the company and the counter-party know exactly what it is they are trying to accomplish. Once a business agreement has been reached, at that time it makes sense to bring in the attorney to draft the legal agreement.

Patent Filing

Patent work is another area where outside legal fees can be slashed with no adverse impact. When filing patents, a great deal of the preliminary work requires researching "prior art." The government website, *uspto.gov*, makes this research very easy, such that administrative staff within the company can perform it for about $20 per hour, compared with a patent attorney doing the same work for $400 per hour. Obviously, once the company has created its dossier of what prior art exists and what the original claims being made are, then it is time to bring in the professional to present the filing application.

Finally, the best way to keep legal fees under control is to have a corporate policy that states that before any outside attorney is retained, all such requests for services will be subject to prior approval by the CFO, and attorney time will be closely monitored. An estimate of time required by the attorney firm should be sought in advance and compared with actual time incurred. Beware of the practice of having two attorneys listen in to a phone call or attend a meeting. As the economy has soured, this practice has tended to be on the rise. In most cases, you, the client, are told that you have the benefit of two minds instead of one, but the attorney firm is the true beneficiary—it is they who are able to raise their gross fees!

If you apply all the recommendations identified above, it should be possible to reduce legal fees by about 50 percent.

Risk Management and 50 percent Reduction of Insurance Expense

Flying a small plane can be dangerous and involves risk. If you crash, you are most likely to die or be critically injured. Regrettably, life insurance companies raise premiums for pilots because of this risk, even though as a population overall, I believe there is an offsetting reduction in the risk of dying from medical complaints—pilots have to undergo regular physicals, which catch complications early on!

The risks from personal flying result predominantly from pilots getting themselves into situations beyond their experience level. For example, a VFR pilot flying into instrument conditions or simply from failing to heed warning signs along the way and not turning back as the weather deteriorates. Good risk management, in this situation, would dictate that a certain pre-determined reduction in visibility would cause a pilot to change his plans.

Risk management is as important in business as it is in flying. It involves:

- Identifying the risk factors,

- Analyzing the effects they will have on your plans,
- Identifying alternative mitigating solutions,

- Choosing the most appropriate solution,

- And implementing it!

If you are flying toward bad weather, the first step in risk management is to recognise that continuing on is not good—nor smart. An analysis performed by scanning the visible horizon might indicate that the area covered by the bad weather will prevent you from reaching your destination. Your alternative solutions are usually to land at an alternate airport nearby to wait out the weather, or return to base.

The initial risk could have been reduced by obtaining a weather forecast before taking off (proper planning), and then, forewarned, not taking off.

"Captain...we're flying completely under the radar!"

In business you want to take steps to minimize the risks, and the rest of this chapter discusses ways to do so.

Insurance covers many areas—typically one thinks of liability and fire as the primary coverages. But a typical portfolio of insurance coverage will probably include Directors and Officers, Workers Compensation, Fire, Theft, Auto, Product Liability, Fiduciary, Errors and Omissions, Export Risk, Non-owned Employee Vehicles, and many more subcategories of risk including terrorism!

When reviewing insurance requirements and options, it is best to recognize that in general, the short term financial interests of your insurance broker are not aligned completely with yours. There is a high probability that the greater the amount of coverage you purchase, the more commission the broker will generate for himself. However, forward thinking brokers who are seeking long-term professional relationships with their clients, and which will lead to referrals for their business, are aware of the ideas discussed below. They should be prompted to evaluate them with you. This is your company, and your money—you lead the way.

It is critical that you become knowledgeable about how risks are rated in general terms so that you can appropriately determine the amount of coverage that is in your best interests. One highly efficient way to do this is to attend the American Management Association's full day course "How to Audit Your Insurance Broker." This is a comprehensive program which describes all the factors which go into rating a particular risk and gives you suggestions about how to reduce them. The course costs about $3,000, and depending on how over-insured you are, may provide you with sufficient knowledge to reduce your premiums by 50 percent.

The overriding concern for purchasing third party insurance is to insure for risks to the company's profitability which you cannot control; risks such as earthquakes, or risks which would cause a major financial problem for the company. An example would be the loss of a brand new $100,000 vehicle.

For insignificant risks, such as the write-off of a 20 year old vehicle with a blue book value of $700, or a shipping loss of a $2,000 computer, it is far more effective to self-insure (i.e., bear the risk of loss yourself). How do you do this? How do you evaluate such risks in order to judge that it makes sense to self insure? There are several areas to probe.

Casualty Loss

The first thing to do is to ask your broker for a loss retention report for the last five to seven years. This will identify every claim you have made on your policies and the values paid out on the claims. You will probably be surprised to see that most claims are for trivial amounts —perhaps a few thousand dollars for a damaged delivery truck, or a lap top computer stolen from an airplane's overhead bin.

Using this data, you can determine an average annual loss and the maximum historical annual loss. The chances are very high that your maximum loss will be less than $20,000 and your average probably less than $10,000.

The next thing to do is to review the policies under which claims were made and make a note of the deductible and the premium for that particular policy. Then contact your broker and ask for a range of premium calculations for increasing deductibles, until the highest deductible offered exceeds at least the average of past years claims, and possibly exceeds the largest claim made.

By raising the deductible above the level of past claims, it will be likely that the premium savings to be achieved will exceed the amount of money received from insurance to settle your claims. This is now a new starting point for your insurance requirements.

Fire/Facilities

Do you know how your fire risk premium is calculated? Many factors are considered, including proximity to fire stations, fire hydrants, flammability of materials in your building and sources of ignition, for example, are you welding? What about sources of fuel—do you store liquid petroleum products, is your building made of wood, etc.? *The most important thing to know is that if you do not tell your broker about why you are not a high fire risk, they will assume that you are and charge accordingly.*

As an example of how lack of communication can penalize you, one manufacturing client of mine had incurred insurance premiums well into six figures—severely out of line with what I believed that particular market to warrant. When I called the broker to help me understand why the premiums were so high, he told me that the buildings had no fire protection (sprinkler systems). Looking up from my desk, I explained that I could see two sprinkler heads in my office and that he must be mistaken at which point he told me the story about how he had asked my predecessor many times for engineering drawings of the building's sprinkler systems to no avail.

I ended the call and walked across to engineering and asked them if they had drawings. As you would expect, with an under-performing company, the answer was "no" which is probably where the previous CFO had ended his quest. But I prevailed upon the VP of Engineering to create the plans within a two week time-frame. Once they were ready, I called the broker to ask about shipping them to him. His response surprised me; he didn't need to see them! He simply reduced the fire premium by $57,000 per year. That was a great return on investment for two man-weeks of engineering time.

Workers Compensation

Most executives think of Workers Compensation as government mandated, arbitrary and capricious, and as being unable to be controlled.

Nothing could be further from the truth. In many companies, 50 percent savings are not uncommon, if you understand how risk ratings are set and you take action to minimize the risks.

Workers Compensation is supposed to be money paid out to workers for injuries they sustain "on the job." Of course, it is well known that many "Monday morning injuries" really occurred during the employees' recreational activities at the weekend, but barring claims on Mondays, how do companies minimize their premiums?

The first thing to know is that your company has an "experience ratio," a history of workers compensation claims paid out. In general, manufacturing occupations are more dangerous than sedentary, and the more workers you have operating heavy machinery, the greater the likelihood of accidents.

Apart from getting out of manufacturing, how then do you reduce your insurance rates?

1. *Reduce the numbers of accidents to zero to reduce your experience ratio.* Make the environment a culture of safety. Go above and beyond the government's (OSHA) requirements for safety devices and notices. Do not tolerate horseplay or bravado around machinery and make such behavior a firing offense.

   Machinery will always win in a game of chicken; it is just a question of time. This is a "skewed odds" situation, where your chance of losing may only be one in a hundred thousand, but if you lose, you lose your life. I was once made aware of a situation in a sawmill where the circular saws moved down lines of timber in a manner similar to "the gauntlet," that medieval contraption of swinging obstructions that people had to time perfectly to get through unharmed. The workers in this sawmill had decided to enliven their days by running between the saws as they moved down the line. Unfortunately, one day, one of the employees tripped as he was running and did not emerge from the other side. While the company was not held liable, because the employees had disregarded warning notices and had climbed over OSHA approved safety guards to play their game, it was not a good day for anyone.

In 20-20 hindsight, and irrespective of the legal liability for such an accident, it is probable that in the situation described above, supervisors either knew and tacitly approved of, or should have known about what was going on. While a supervisor cannot be standing guard all the time, and should not have to, if management had made the culture of safety "Job 1," and had had zero tolerance for anyone disregarding safety rules or equipment, the accident may not have happened.

2. *Demonstrate your commitment to safety by having a written safety policy, appointing a safety officer, and holding frequent training sessions.* Set the tone at the management level by always complying with safety notices and penalize anyone who is caught disobeying the safety rules e.g. not wearing safety glasses or hard hats in areas where these are needed. Provide incentives to employees for every month the company is accident free.

3. *Ensure that classifications of employees are correct.* Do not allow the insurer to classify as manufacturing employees staff who may simply work within the manufacturing department such as cost accountants, inside sales or purchasing agents. These people sit at desks, and do not operate machinery. As sedentary employees, their insurance rates should be less than half of the rates charged on machinery operators. Do not allow inside sales people, commission administrators or others who never leave the office be classified as outside sales people, as this classification is also highly rated.

4. *Apply all the rules regarding payroll management from Chapter 4, Zero Tolerance for Error.* Simply having a drug-free policy should reduce your premiums by 20 percent.

5. *Require that any employee who will be driving on company business has a DUI free traffic record.* No exceptions.

6. *If you have had a downsizing or payroll reduction, ensure that you are correctly classifying your wages by department.* Most Workers Compensation insures base their rates on anticipated gross payroll, and then perform an audit after the fact, adjusting premiums up or down from what was expected. However, sometimes, an audit may not take place. If you have made significant changes, you may want to request an early audit, or at the very least, ensure that an audit takes place after the premium year end so that you can obtain a premium rebate.

Introducing all of the above has a very high likelihood of reducing your Workers Compensation premiums by 50 percent, as well as leading tangentially to higher quality output and less absenteeism. It is all related to what gets measured that actually gets accomplished.

Vehicles

If your company owns vehicles, don't insure them for every peril. Have at least a $1,000 and preferably a higher deductible on them. Make the drivers responsible for any damage they cause. And don't cover older vehicles for comprehensive or collision—the premium will be greater than any potential claim once a vehicle is more than 6 years old. Require DMV reports on all drivers, and as discussed in Chapter 11, *Don't be Taken for a Ride—Transportation Costs*, make DUI a firing offense. Consider defensive driver training courses for all company drivers—the premium reductions often outweigh the costs of such courses.

Fiduciary Coverage

Always perform credit checks on any employee who will have financial responsibility. You do not want to have anyone in the accounting department who has personal financial problems because any controls can ultimately be circumvented by knowledgeable insiders.

International Operations

Chapter 13, *Turnarounds in the International Arena*, provides a great deal of insight on how American companies can become more profitable internationally, but the key thing to remember regarding insurance is that to the extent possible, you should place your overseas risks in overseas markets. US insurers will base their international premiums not only on the actual potential insured loss, but also take account of what would happen in the event of a lawsuit against the company and any awards of damages, many of which bear no relationship to the harm suffered.

While the risk of lawsuits is significant in the US, it is primarily a US-only risk. Insuring overseas operations to the same level makes no sense where lawsuits are neither common nor likely to succeed. If your US company likes centralized operations, then working with a major international brokerage should resolve this problem. If it does not, then allow each overseas subsidiary to apply the above principles of premium reduction and then obtain a local quote.

How to Really Save Insurance Money—But Only if You Are Large and Profitable—Captive Insurance Companies

If you are a large company whose revenues exceed $100 million, you earn profits of more than $1.2 million, and you are very risk conscious and have a very low loss history, it may make a great deal of financial sense to set up a Captive Insurance Company. To do so, you should talk to one of the professional firms specializing is such operations.

The principle is straight forward. Your company sets up "Insurance Subsidiary, Inc." as a separate company in which you own 100 percent of the shares. You pay premiums to your Captive. Your Captive pays out any losses. In order to avoid catastrophic losses, the Captive takes out a policy at Lloyds of London for losses in excess of what it itself can pay out. And any surplus in the Captive is free of tax! Under current tax laws, you can pay up to $1.2 million in premiums to your Captive, which can then pay out any profits as dividends. The effect is to convert ordinary income to dividend income saving up to 25 percent in taxes.

Conclusion

A focus on safety and personal responsibility will bring down insurance rates substantially. Seeing this focus by management will lead to productivity improvements elsewhere as the culture of the company changes for the better. Always verify that your broker knows about all risk mitigation your company undertakes, and maximize all deductibles. Self insure for minor risks, and set up a Captive if circumstances allow.

CHAPTER 8

How to Win the Sweepstakes

Treasury Management

Traditional Definition of a Bank: A place which will lend you money provided you can give them sufficient evidence that you don't need it. If you are a business which has fallen on hard times, you will not get help here! In fact, the bank might hasten your journey into oblivion by calling in your loans.

2006-7 Definition of a Bank: A place that will throw money at you to put into shoddily built houses even if you have no intention of keeping them. Unless you are into building houses, you will find it difficult to get a loan.

2011 Definition of a Bank: A place which is calling in all its cash and not lending anyone anything because it is afraid the government will require stiffer capital requirements than heretofore. You are unlikely to get a loan!

So how do we work with these organizations for a win-win outcome? In exactly the same way that pilots and air traffic controllers do—a relationship that inspires and relies on trust. In the air, the relationship between pilots and controllers is cemented by the very first air to air communication. On the ground, in business it is between the CFO and the Bank's Lending Officer.

A few years ago, I was flying my plane all the way south along the west coast between Seattle and San Francisco on what had been forecast to be a clear day for the entire journey. This was an important consideration, as I was flying VFR (visual flight rules, where it is the pilot's responsibility to see and be seen and avoid any other traffic or obstacles). By the time I was about 60 miles north of San Francisco, I could see the fog rolling in and realized that I would not be able to complete my journey unless I changed my flight plan to IFR (instrument flight rules, where you are allowed to fly in the clouds with controllers directing your altitude, heading and speed). Checking my exact position, and maintaining straight and level flight, I called up Northern California Approach Control, the body responsible for all air traffic approaching the Bay Area, and stated, in my best pilot speak, "NorCal Approach, Skylane 129SE 60 miles north of San Francisco, 9,500, VFR to San Carlos, request IFR clearance." Within a couple of minutes of my call, ATC had identified me, given me a discrete squawk code, and begun vectoring me into the fog and ultimately to a landing at San Carlos, about 10 miles south of the San Francisco International Airport (SFO).

A few minutes after I had received my clearance, another pilot, probably in a similar situation to me called up, and in a halting, amateurish and confused manner, made a similar request. The Controller's response was a terse "unable." I fully expected a debate to ensue on the airwaves as to why I had just received a clearance for a similar request, but it didn't. Perhaps the other pilot was secretly glad that he had been denied permission to fly into the clouds.

Why had I been approved for my flight and the other pilot denied? Because I used the magic words, in the order they were expected by the Controller, and I exuded confidence that I was capable of complying with his instructions. When one of the radio calls I heard as I passed, in the clouds, over the approach from the south to SFO, was to warn a descending 747 that the traffic 1000 feet above him one mile away, was me travelling west, I realized that the entire air traffic control system is built on trust—the Controller trusted me to maintain altitude and heading so I would be no factor to the 747 and I trusted the Controller to vector me to avoid anything else in the clouds.

Approaching the Bank

We have to approach the banks in the same way. We have to exude confidence that our company will be a winner. We have to use banker's magic words, which are usually positive cash flow, increased profits, maintaining covenants, and we have to convince them through our actions that we will do what we said and comply with those covenants. We are not 501(c)(3) charities expecting corporate donations, and banks are not philanthropic organizations. Banks (used to) exist to make money for their shareholders, by lending money for more than it costs them to borrow from savers. Corporations borrow the bank's money in order to make a greater return on that capital than it costs to borrow from the banks. One feeds the other. *Our job as Corporate CFO or CEO is to use banks to our advantage by convincing them they will make money from us.*

Where can we start? Most distressed companies have very little cash and too much debt. Surprisingly, they also often tend to have many more operating accounts than would be warranted for the size of their operations, and a large number of small loans, probably taken out at times when they had a small amount of borrowing capacity. These cash accounts, usually with petty amounts in them, and loan accounts, often with small principal balances perhaps representing the last year or so of a five year loan, make it difficult to keep track of exactly how much cash and debt a company has at its disposal. Having multiple accounts might also make it impossible to meet obligations which if accounts were combined, would be covered. For example, a company having cash balances of $500,000 in each of two separate operating accounts, for a total of $1 million of available cash would not be able to honor a standing order for payroll of $750,000 to be withdrawn from one of those accounts.

Even though the company has the total cash available to meet its payroll requirements, the location of the cash is not where it needs to be, and if such a situation occurred in real life, and employees were not paid, no matter what explanation the company provided, people would begin to get worried and rumors could fly. Before you could control it, a self-inflicted downward spiral could begin as rumors of financial insecurity spread and employees left.

Because a culture of overall lack of control leads to profitability problems, there is a high probability that in an underperforming company, senior management is not aware of exactly how much cash and debt a company has, nor how it is distributed. And only a few banks will advise their clients on how best to minimize the costs of all that debt.

It is often the case that there are accounts and loans at multiple banks. This might be for historical reasons such as convenience of depositing checks, or a requirement that a bank had when taking out a loan, that an operating account be opened at that bank as well. Other frequent reasons for having multiple accounts are to segregate cash for payroll, benefits, direct deposits, etc.

The number one priority is to identify all operating accounts and aggregate them into one major account. There may still be a value to having a small petty cash disbursement account, but the need for other accounts should be carefully scrutinized. This cuts down the need for administrative work in the form of monthly reconciliations, and makes it easy to understand exactly how much cash the company owns at any point in time.

On the loan side of the equation, a company in difficulties may not have just one revolving line, it perhaps may have a fixed asset loan, a receivables loan, and a working capital line. The ideal goal is to aggregate all debt at the lowest possible interest rate so that only one monthly payment is required. Therefore, all loans should be identified, together with their terms and covenants. Covenant control worksheets should be created. The biggest problems in terms of creating covenant control worksheets arise with loans which have been renegotiated so many times they are now up to their "Eighth Amendment." If you are starting from scratch in creating the covenant control worksheet, this can be especially difficult if each amendment refers to prior amendments!

Actual Debt and Net Debt

In terms of debt, there may also be outstanding balances on company credit cards, travel agent accounts, fuel company management, and leasing.

The costs associated with such a spread of the assets and liabilities is not simply the administrative headaches of reconciling each one every month, (although in a badly managed company, such reconciliations are unlikely to be performed!). They include maintenance fees, and by far the largest cost, interest on all outstanding debt which may be being calculated on loan principal as much as two, three or four times the actual NET debt of the company.

What is net debt? Suppose the company has a cash operating account which fluctuates around a monthly average of $1 million. After a bi-weekly payroll withdrawal it may sink as low as $100,000, and sometimes after large customer deposits, may rise as high as $2 million. This same company also has a working capital line of credit of $2 million outstanding, which has required monthly payments of interest only—at 14 percent. The annual interest on this line will be $280,000.

But the NET debt averages only $1 million—i.e. the loan balance of $2 million less the average cash on hand of $1 million. That means your actual interest rate, i.e. the interest charge of $280,000 represents an annual rate of 28 percent on your NET debt. Remember, on average, you have $1 million of cash on hand, (in today's environment earning nothing in interest) yet your credit line stays at $2 million borrowed.

How do you create a situation where you are only paying interest, and only on the net debt? The answer is a "Sweep Account." In such an account, at the end of the day, all cash on hand is "swept" into the "line of credit" account, reducing the balance on which interest is calculated for that night.

By setting up such a program, the interest is only then charged on the net debt of $1 million. In this example, the company saves $140,000 per year in interest charges. Not all banks offer this option,

as they too can do the math and understand that your interest savings of $140,000 represents less profit to them. Therefore, it is imperative that you find a bank that will offer this service. If you are unable to find such a bank, because of your circumstances or location, then you can to a certain extent "create" your own sweep account.

This requires a responsible Controller, and an Internet, real-time bank connection allowing access to all deposit and loan accounts. At the end of the banking day, every day, the Controller accesses the company's balance, and transfers the available cash balance to the loan account. The following morning, money is transferred back out to take care of the day's disbursements.

If there are multiple loans outstanding, with different maturity dates, and different interest rates, etc., the goal should be to consolidate as quickly as possible. Not only will this simplify administration, it is possible that the ability of the company to borrow may increase if monthly payments can be reduced because of a consolidation of loans into one larger, and further out maturity.

Be aware of interest rates. Today's environment of generally low interest rates means that there is a fairly high likelihood that you could obtain a lower rate on your borrowings than you are paying on loans taken out more than three years ago. This may also be especially possible if former loans were taken out at "distressed" pricing but under your new "12-step plan to profitability" you now you have a decent business plan. If your loan was taken out under asset based lending because you weren't profitable, and now you are, a revolving line may make more sense.

Be aware of covenants. Banks like to set these tight. The tighter they are, the more likelihood you will breach one, which gives the bank an opportunity to call in the loan if they so desire—a major problem for the company. More likely, they will charge you a covenant waiver fee, pricey but not disastrous. The more generous the covenants you can negotiate up front, the more flexibility you will have and a lower overall cost of debt.

Company credit cards should be avoided. It is too easy for employees who perhaps do not have purchasing authority to charge something to the card. These purchases may or may not be legitimate, but without a second person reviewing them, and without the Controller knowing what is going out, they are avenues of leakage for cash. There is nothing which could be acquired by a company credit card which a company can't do without for the couple more days required to process a Purchase Order or send a company check for Cash on Delivery.

Bank Speak for Financial Controllers

In order to obtain the best possible terms on a loan, good financial accounting is required. It is imperative that financial statements are produced in a timely manner, and that receivables are adequately managed. The bank also likes to see the output from the subject of Chapter 1, *It's Always in the Numbers, Always*, of this book, the 13-week, (and full year) Cash Flow Forecast. This forecast must show that profitability will be achieved, and subsequent reporting must show progress being made towards this goal.

Conclusion

Consolidate your cash and consolidate your loans. A history of meeting scheduled payments, and of meeting forecasts, will work wonders when it comes time to renegotiating debt, to more favorable terms. Such terms are in your hands.

CHAPTER 9

Pay Me Now or Pay Me Later

Purchasing, Inventory and Manufacturing— Working with All the Stakeholders

Blowout on the Runway

Every pilot has his share of mishaps, and the hope is that they are sufficiently small that they do no significant or permanent damage to either the pilot or the airplane. One of mine happened on a day when I was landing at Durango, and, in an effort to be courteous to a jet which was landing close behind, I applied full brakes so as to be able to turn off the runway at the first taxiway connector. Unfortunately, I locked my wheels and a tire blew out, causing some interesting comments from the FBO (Fixed Base Operator, the General Aviation Terminal Manager), who saw what had happened and thought I would run off the runway.

Immediately, I informed the jet of the situation, even though they had probably already begun their $1,000 go-around, meaning that they would abort the landing and enter into a holding pattern. I called for assistance from the FBO, and kept the commercial jet updated on what we were doing. Once we had an idea of how long it would take us to clear the runway, I was able to communicate this to the jet, so that they knew they could hold for a while longer without having to return to Denver. With three of us lifting the wing so that the wheel strut could be placed on a wheeled dolly, we were able to push my plane off the runway in just a few minutes, allowing the jet to land, and everyone who saw us to have a good laugh!

This rapid resolution came about because all the stakeholders worked together. I wanted to get off the runway as quickly as possible so that the jet did not have to return to Denver, disappointing passengers on it, and waiting for the return flight. The FBO wanted the jet on the ground so they could refuel it. The jet's pilots wanted to be on the ground so their schedule wouldn't be disrupted. By communicating what we were doing and the estimated time requirements, we were all able to accomplish our objectives.

In turn-around situations, sometimes the best laid plans suffer a blowout. Perhaps a delivery isn't made when it should be, or a customer payment is not received. Perhaps machinery breaks down or a key person leaves. Under all of these circumstances, it is better to communicate to all affected parties the changes to the plan which will be necessary to overcome the new obstacle.

It is also good to know the limits of what actions can be taken and how you can influence them. No amount of verbal abuse from the cockpit of the jet would have made my plane move any more quickly off the runway. Likewise, in a situation where you simply don't have the cash to make a scheduled payment, no amount of threats from vendors can change that. But keeping them in the loop about your intentions will probably save a lot of aggravation.

What actions can we take to reduce the need to miss payments to suppliers as we are turning around our corporation? What follows are the answers.

Supplier Payment Terms—2% 10 days, Net 30 days

Heretic (n) - a holder of opinions contrary to conventional belief.

In order to make money on purchasing you need to be a heretic! You need to pay your suppliers with urgency! Take advantage of any 2/10, net 30 terms. (This means that suppliers assume you will pay within 30 days, but if you pay within 10 days, they will give you a two percent discount.) By paying early, you are gaining a 36 percent return on your capital. If you don't have the cash, but you are able to borrow, you should even take out a line of credit from your bank at usurious rates (within limits) in order to pay your suppliers and take advantage of this discount. Some banks are even offering lines of credit with the express purpose of doing just this!

How is this 36 percent rate of return calculated? Assuming you are a good, responsible customer, dealing with normal suppliers, under normal payment terms, you will pay those suppliers 30 days after invoice date. If, by taking advantage of 2/10, you will pay them 20 days sooner, you save two percent of the invoice price. And that's without having an exceptional purchasing manager! It increases your gross margin (based on cost of materials) by two percent.

Looked at another way, if you had chosen not to pay the supplier until the remaining 20 days allowed by the terms were up, you would have had to earn an additional two percent in those 20 days on the money not sent to the supplier. Earning two percent in 20 days is equivalent to an interest rate of 36 percent per year. Where else can you get such a risk-free rate of return? You can't.

It makes sense to borrow against your line of credit to pay your suppliers early, assuming your interest rate is less than 36 percent.

But wait—there's more!

By paying extremely promptly, you are demonstrating to your suppliers a track record of paying promptly, so there is now a very good chance that your purchasing manager will be able to negotiate even keener prices. Why? Because by maintaining prompt payments, you are demonstrating financial strength. Your supplier will believe there is less risk that you will go bankrupt. So he won't have to price that risk into what he charges you. He won't have to price in delayed payments, cost of collection, his own negative impact on working capital, and sleepless nights caused by the concern that if you don't pay, he might not make payroll. So he will be very happy to keep you happy. I have found it to be not uncommon to be able to negotiate five to ten percent price reductions from regular suppliers by demonstrating a track record of consistent early payments.

This advice is contrary to conventional wisdom that you should drag out payments as long as possible, but the time wasted by purchasing staff fielding phone calls from aggrieved suppliers who want to get paid after you exceed 30 days has costs. Benefits of prompt payment far exceed those imagined by dragging it out, especially in days of virtually zero interest rates.

Inventory Levels Too High

In all of my manufacturing turnaround successes, a major problem initially was inventory levels being way too high. And this occurred in companies even where the purchasing manger was a successful trader (lumber) or a great negotiator (bulk chemicals).

Let's look at the lumber industry first. My client was a reseller of lumber for the house building industry. It bought lumber by the car load and resold by the stick. Lumber is a commodity which trades on the futures exchange. It is fairly predictable, both seasonally and within limited ranges. The purchasing manager had been a trader on the exchange, before getting "burned out," but still was sufficiently skilled, that as an actual physical user, he was consistently buying at the low points of the price cycle. There were two problems with this however. When I was brought in, the sales volume of the company was declining to 50 percent of the prior year. Yet the minimum quantities this trader was buying were as high as in the prior year. And while he was certainly getting in at the low points of the short cycle, prices for the previous year had been, and continued to be in a massive down trend—the lows kept getting lower, and he was swamped with inventory at the higher price.

While this man was doing everything which had historically enabled his company to be highly profitable, this same behavior was now leading its downfall—on two fronts.

I had no idea you could save so much MONEY!

He had failed to acknowledge that the increasing sales volumes he had seen in the 2004 – 2006 period were in fact an aberration, and were now declining significantly. Even though he had daily sales figures, and moving averages, all of which were pointing downwards, he failed to adjust his inventory levels down. As a result, he had inventory which now reflected four months of sales, in an industry which could easily restock in two to four weeks. The fix was to put an immediate stop on all purchasing until stocks of everything other than the most frequently used items were down to two weeks. We figured that because all the other lumber yards in the area were facing the same problems, if we were out of stock on something one of our regular customers suddenly needed, we could obtain it from a competitor at a price hardly any greater than if we had originally bought wholesale.

The second problem was obsolescence. While the "average" level of inventory was now four months, due to the collapse of the top end of the housing market, many of the specialist types of wood, for cabinetry or floors, were now being held at two years supply. The cost of holding inventory in terms of insurance, and worse, in the case of wood, its weathering (if left untreated outside), or damage and warehousing costs (if inside), has been estimated to be about one quarter of the original value annually.

Another egregious example of bulk purchasing gone awry was observed in a bulk chemicals distributor. In this example, the client used 10,000 gallons of a product every month. The purchasing manager, knowing that the product was always going to be a best seller, negotiated a bulk purchase deal with the supplier for buying 50,000 gallons at a time. What he failed to take into account was that the cost of storing 50,000 gallons of this chemical was more than five times the cost of storing 10,000 gallons of fluid because of EPA regulations, in addition to the larger tanks needed.

When we reviewed these costs, we found that we would have been much better off just ordering 10,000 gallons at a time. Because this chemical was a mainstay of the enterprise, and we assumed that we would continue to sell 10,000 gallons per month, the supplier was approached for a bulk discount price based on a minimum commitment of 100,000 gallons per year, to be delivered in 10,000 gallon increments when we wanted it. Not only did we maintain our discount, we increased it because it was easier for the manufacturer to deliver us 10,000 gallons at a time than arranging for a 50,000 gallon delivery. This really was a win-win situation. And it freed up over $100,000 of working capital for us—in an $8 million revenue company.

Getting Cozy with Purchasing Managers

Everyone's favorite radio station is WIIFM—What's In It For Me? Regrettably, at some companies, for a purchasing manager, it is the amount rebated in person to that purchasing manager. Office supplies are an area where scams abound. I have come across toner cartridges which would retail for $100 at an office supply store being sold at $300 each to an office manager who then received high value gift cards to electronics stores.

It is absolutely critical that a CFO periodically look at the original invoices for purchases in order to ensure that a company is not being taken for a ride by its own staff. Trust, but verify.

Leased Equipment

In the office itself, there is a high likelihood that machines such as photocopiers are still being leased even after they have no value. In most cases of companies in trouble, equipment has been leased, simply because leasing offered a financing alternative otherwise not available. Because every month, a fixed amount has been deducted from the bank account, no one has really bothered to find out what it was for and whether or not that equipment is needed today. If the equipment is still needed, most office equipment leases have buyout clauses to them, either fair market value, or a nominal residual value at the end of the lease term which will usually be in the range of three to five years. But what happens if you don't exercise your option? The equipment leasing company is usually very happy to keep taking a large sum of money every month for a piece of equipment that is close to worthless!

How to resolve this cash drain? Identify every piece of office equipment which is on a lease and determine if it can be bought out or returned to the manufacturer. And before leasing any new equipment, run complete TCO (total cost of ownership) calculations to determine if it really does make sense to lease or whether or not you should buy outright.

How to Cut Costs in Manufacturing

Cost Accounting Is Irrelevant, Dangerous and Harmful! Yes, you read that correctly.

Traditional cost accounting, where the actual cash costs required to manufacture a product become capitalized and put on the balance sheet, is irrelevant and harmful to the efficient running of a manufacturing operation. It provides no information whatsoever about the true cost of production and can lead to faulty decision making.

Provided below is a very simple example to prove how harmful cost accounting is to general management, which my readers in England will appreciate. It describes a hypothetical Newsagent's shop trying to increase its profitability by adding peanut sales into its offerings. In the old days in England, customers bought newspapers in shops called Newsagents, which usually were small sole proprietorships, in areas of high foot traffic such as close to bus stops, train stations or town centers. They had big flat counters displaying all the newspaper titles.

Additionally, to keep traffic high in the shop throughout the day, these shops usually sold sweets (candies), drinks and maybe stationery and cards.

Here is the situation describing why cost accounting provides inappropriate data on which to make profitability decisions: One afternoon, the proprietor of one of these shops was approached by a peanut salesman, who noticed that not only were his company's peanuts not available for sale, but that a large area of the newsagent's shop's floor space was unused. Pointing out to the owner that his company would provide, free of charge, a display stand for the peanuts, and that the shop owner's mark up on the peanuts was 100%, he persuaded the proprietor to put one of the peanut company's stands on the floor.

After two weeks, the proprietor was exceedingly happy—he was selling an average of $200 per week of peanuts, making an average annual increase in profits of $5,000, or enough to take himself and his wife on a luxury cruise. At the end of the month, he expected his accountant, who prepared his books, to be just as overjoyed, but instead, the accountant sternly told the newsagent that he had to stop selling the peanuts because he was losing money on the sale. Being a simple man, the newsagent, who only saw an increase in his cash of $100 per week, and equated that with profit, could not understand why the accountant was so distraught and asked him patiently to explain. Seeing an opportunity to show off his academic skills, the accountant began to introduce the concept of absorption of overhead. Overhead was all the fixed costs of running the business, the rent, utilities and so on, and in the retail business, the appropriate measurement against which to allocate overhead was by square feet of floor space taken up by the display.

As the peanut stand occupied three square feet of floor space, and the overhead was $50 per week per square foot, the stand received a $150 per week allocation of fixed costs. Because the peanuts were only generating $100 of profit, the transaction was losing $50 per week!

An astute observer will immediately see that the allocation of those $150 of fixed costs to peanuts led to a reduction in allocation to other products such as newspapers, making them "more profitable" to sell. But I present this example because using the data provided and the recommendation generated, while meaning to be simple and humorous, is regrettably what many manufacturing companies still do when they attempt to calculate product profitability. They ignore the fact that overhead does not go away, it merely gets re-allocated, and by absorbing overhead costs into manufacturing costs, overhead is often hidden from day-to-day measurement, and hence no longer is a focus of cost containment.

If you are a manufacturer or a retail business which uses full absorption costing, NO financial decision should be made using this data. Its only relevance is to statutory financial reporting. Hence in terms of costs of running the manufacturing plant, you should be looking at controllable costs such as rent, utilities, wages, costs of materials, maintenance, etc. And if your accounting system does not provide that data, change systems!

The Manufacturing Shop Needs a Plan, and a VP Who Can Schedule

Nothing causes a manufacturing plant's costs to go out of control more than not planning. Changing the product being worked on involves changeover and set-up time—all non-productive cost wasters. And trying to get product out of the door by the 32nd or 33rd of the month to make last month's "numbers" is self destructive. Not only does it rob from next month, it usually requires lots of overtime at time-and-a-half, and inefficiencies in production because of changeover time to get a few specific products complete instead of working on all similar products together.

The most critical requirement for a successful VP of Manufacturing is one who can schedule effectively, tie all his inventory needs into a month's production run, and work a balanced production line with no unnecessary overtime, changeovers, or slack time. This is a long term objective to accomplish, but the overtime ban, discussed previously in Chapter 4, *Zero Tolerance for Error*, will force production changes to be made, if manufacturing has been a large user of overtime historically.

Little Things Add Up

There used to be a saying in England—take care of the pennies and the pounds will take care of themselves. In order to make money, expenses must be taken care of, and in order to ingrain the frugal mentality into the culture, little things matter. For example, lights in rooms no one is in should be turned off. Last person out of the office at night should turn out the lights, and the coffer makers!

In the good old USA, there is no justification for purchasing bottled water—in many cases tap water is in fact purer than the bottled stuff, and there is no transportation system for water more efficient and economical than piping it into a building!

Conclusion

Pay your suppliers early, keep inventory low, and remember that in creating a cost effective mindset, while individually, each of the savings may be small, it shows employees that all expenses matter. It's attitude.

CHAPTER 10

There Is No Margin for Error

Gross Margin Analysis Tells You Where the Leaks Are!

W hy do runways have centerlines? Because if you land your airplane with your nose wheel on the center line, and keep it there, there is a very good chance you will stay on the runway. The FAA sets "Practical Test Standards" for all of the various ratings of pilot certificate, from Private, through Commercial, to Airline Transport. These standards become more exacting and allow for less and less deviation from the centerline on landing as your ratings allow you more privileges. To obtain the private pilot certificate, you have to barely show the FAA that you are capable of landing on a wide strip of tarmac on a calm windless day, but by the time you are an Airline Transport Pilot, you are expected to put the plane down, on the numbers, straight down the center line, in a 30 knot crosswind. And if you have some malfunctioning equipment, or the weather is bad, the skills you have developed in your practice will be called upon, as you need to be precise to obtain that successful landing from which everyone walks away unharmed!

I found that one of the best training grounds for my developing absolute precision skills was in Alaska, where I earned my Seaplane Rating.

The valleys we trained in were so narrow and deep that our distance from the hillside was measured in wingspans rather than hundreds of feet, and the lakes were no more than ponds, meaning we had to put the plane down first time, within a couple of feet of the water's edge.

While landing a conventional plane on a 10,000 foot long runway 150 feet wide will not test your skills, putting a float plane down on a small pond in a narrow box canyon leaves no margin for error.

And so it is in a business. When everything is going fine, no one pays any attention to the details, but that is when the problems begin. The margin for error in landing a plane occurs in three dimensions, vertical rate of descent, lateral drift and speed along the runway. All of these dimensions have recommended limits in order to "stabilize the approach." If you don't have a stable approach, you must go around and try again. But what if you don't recognize that you are not stabilized? Allow any of these measurements to leave their tolerances, and you might run off the runway, tip over, or catch fire. In a business, your tolerances are ensuring that cash coming in exceeds cash going out. Failure to control your margins will lead to you losing money, or in the worst case scenario, going bankrupt.

In a plane, the consequences of coming down too fast or failing to flare before reaching the runway are a collapsed undercarriage, and substantial propeller, engine and airframe damage.

Drift too far laterally, and you might collapse the landing gear from side loads, or go into the mud and tip over. Land too fast and you could run off the end, either crashing through whatever there is at the end of the runway, or stopping in the mud and tipping over!

But get all three parameters right and your passengers will applaud, and you will have a smooth taxi to the gate!

On a runway, the margins for error are the excess width over what you really need to land straight ahead, and the extra length of runway beyond the distance normally required to stop.

In a business, the margin for error is the difference between what it costs you to make something and the price at which you sell it. *The greater the margin, the greater the profit.*

In a stable business, margins should be relatively constant. In a dynamic environment, if the cost of supplies has increased, without a corresponding increase in your sales price, or increase in efficiency, your margins will be squeezed. And conversely, if you have become more productive and found ways to reduce costs without reducing prices to customers, your margins will increase.

Therefore, by understanding the individual components of your business, you should have a very good idea of the margin trends you would expect. Most executives in underperforming companies believe they have a "seat of the pants" knowledge of where their profits come from. But as we've shown in the flying example in Chapter 1, *It's Always in the Numbers, Always*, flying by the seat of your pants in the clouds leads to a death spiral. So it is with margin expectations—the seat of the pants expectations may be totally wrong in practice. You can only confirm your expectations by performing a gross margin analysis frequently. If the results are not what you would expect, then you will need to perform more diligence to determine what is causing the unexpected reduction, (and it always is a reduction) in the margins you would have anticipated.

To show how powerful margin analysis is in its ability to keep a company within the tolerances needed for success, I present below an example from a client where negligent management and multiple control failures had allowed criminal activity to defraud the company.

Cash for Chemicals

The company was a bulk chemicals distribution firm. While revenues had remained relatively constant over the previous few years, the company was rapidly losing money. Through questioning, observation and review of basic financial, purchasing and sales documents, I had gained a thorough understanding of the trends and competitive pressures in this business. It appeared that over the three years prior to my arrival, the company had enjoyed a great ability to raise prices because of its strong position in the local market in terms of exceptional customer service. Additionally, because the company's purchasing manager was a wily negotiator, and they were willing to sole source major bulk chemicals, input prices had declined.

Therefore, even though I had already identified gross over-staffing throughout the company, total lack of control of receivables, excess inventory of hardware, and just about every other problem identified in "The 12-Step Plan," for the reasons above, I fully expected to see a fairly reasonable improvement in the gross margins obtained by the company in this three year time frame. The exercise I performed was,

"Did anyone check the fuel before takeoff?"

at the outset, one of curiosity rather than investigation, because I had assumed that with the numerous other problems the company had, here at least would be a positive sign which, once we had sorted out everything else, would be the road to profitability.

How wrong I was. The analysis was extremely simple to begin with. For each of the 36 months prior to my arrival, I simply obtained the monthly gross revenues from chemical sales. This excluded service charges, hardware, tax, and ancillary services. For cost of sales, I simply added up the costs of all the purchases of bulk chemicals. Note—there was no inventory management system and no one had bothered to try to match sales with purchases—however, on balance, purchases were relatively smooth. I was calculating these numbers monthly and then adding them up to create a 12 month moving average, as this would smooth out purchase volume fluctuations.

My numbers now allowed me to produce two lines on a graph— the top line representing a trailing 12 month average of chemicals revenues, and the bottom line a trailing 12 month average of chemicals purchases. I had already looked at unit sales and purchase prices of a sample of the chemicals this company dealt with, and based on these numbers, was expecting the revenues line to slope upwards at a greater angle than the cost line, generating increasing margins as the lines diverged and increasing from about 45 percent three years ago to 55 percent today. What I found shocked me and caused me to re-run the numbers. The most recent margin, according to this analysis, had dropped to 35 percent.

Having verified that the data were correct, it was time to find the cause of the problem. The first place to look was the transfer yard. Here, bulk chemicals in three thousand gallon or greater storage tanks were disbursed into 35 gallon drums, or used to fill up smaller tanks on the backs of flat-bed trucks which would then visit work sites to refill containers there. What I found shocked me. The delivery meters from the large tanks, if they could be found, were either caked in grime and could not be read, or were inoperative or missing. No one had read these meters in years.

The smaller delivery truck meters were in the same condition. No one read those either. Why bother—it was a family company, everyone had worked there for years, and the only control needed was the sales invoices ... wasn't it? Assuming that when small drums were dropped off, or a customer's tank refilled, wouldn't the sales invoice tell my client how much chemical had been used? Why bother with trying to fix meters, read numbers, and fill out paperwork, especially if some of the drivers were just marginally literate?

Obviously, I am being a little sarcastic to make the point that reconciliations are valuable. But in this case, even taking into account that no one was reading what was discharged from the bulk tanks, and no one was counting the barrels, a divergence from the expected margin of 20 percentage points was too large to be put down to not quite matching what came out of the big tanks to what went in to the small drums.

What might the answer be? As a cynical ex-auditor who was taught to consider every possible opportunity for fraud, the logical explanation was that employees were stealing the chemicals. But why—they are bulky, dirty, and difficult to sell on eBay. So how might the fraud be taking place?

The only way to find out, even with GPS mounted on the trucks (see Chapter 11, *Don't be Taken for a Ride—Transportation Costs*), was to observe. Through getting to know most of the staff, I had determined through my "auditor's nose" who I thought the "wide boys" (a British term for less than honest person) might be. So one morning, I waited in the parking lot opposite the yard for my selected victim to drive out. Driving my everyman, plain rental car, it was not difficult to blend into the busy traffic. Plus, I had a rough idea of where he was going as I had requested a print-out from the dispatcher of all the scheduled delivery runs for that day (no need to raise suspicions by asking for just one!). Once at his first stop, I chose a vantage point in the strip center opposite and watched the interaction between the delivery driver and his customer. I made a note of the number of barrels off-loaded and their colors, watched the driver and the customer share a laugh and a smoke together, saw the driver tear off a delivery note, and saw what looked like cash changing hands. This was surprising as all our customers were on account, and invoices were created within 24 hours of delivery from the delivery notes handed in by the drivers at the end of each day's deliveries.

Now it was time to get back on the road to follow the driver to the next customer. A similar situation repeated itself. This happened four more times before the deliveries were done.

I went back to my hotel and tallied up what I expected the deliveries to total, based on my observations of the colored barrels. The next day, back at the office, I asked the sales accountant for the delivery reports from the previous day's deliveries, found my driver's list, and compared quantities. I was shocked to find that what he had provided to her for billing purposes showed about 33 percent fewer barrels than I had observed. This was why the cash was changing hands.

If one guy was doing it, perhaps the whole staff was doing it. They had realized that there were no controls and were taking advantage of a family, trusting environment.

Action was required to stop this right now ... and the best part about performing turn arounds is that action MUST be performed right now, otherwise the business will fail. The owner and I knew what we had to do before the drivers returned at the end of the day. The first thing was to replace all the broken volume meters on the storage tanks and small delivery trucks. Next we had to mandate that the service manager's first priority of the day was to note every discharge from the storage tanks into the barrels and the smaller trucks. And from the next morning, every truck going out and coming back was going to have its barrels of chemicals inventoried as it left and arrived back at the yard. We were going to have a controlled yard just like Hertz!

Finally, we had called our "chemicals-for-cash" employee and asked that he meet us at the end of his shift.

Employees were shocked by the sudden lock down. They immediately realized that the gravy train was ending. And when they realized the following day that one of their brethren was no longer with them, a few more changes would soon work themselves out.

Our culprit was confronted with the observations from the prior day concerning cash, and barrels delivered not agreeing with the number of barrels on his invoice sheet. He admitted guilt and was terminated. There was no need to prolong the debate by pursuing criminal charges. Our own lack of records would have made it very difficult to prove a case without a reasonable doubt in any case, but as the staff now knew we knew, the problem would not continue.

The message had been transmitted and understood by the rest of the employees. As expected, the remaining bad apples left. They either feared that we had caught them too and were just taking our time to terminate them, or had the data to do so, or because they realized that their chances of being able to sell our product for cash to customers was now almost impossible, and therefore the job didn't hold the same excitement or money making opportunities for them!

Lo and behold, margins moved rapidly toward the expected 55 percent. But other benefits, unexpected by the company's owners, but fully anticipated by me, took place. The staff that remained, the honest ones, were happy to know that they were now in a majority and that now the company could perhaps recognize them. But also, because there was no need to do "behind the bike shed" deals, delivery times dropped, and an average run of four to five deliveries per day typically became eight stops. We were able to make the same amount of deliveries with fewer staff and fewer trucks, so not only did reported gross margin increase, overhead was massively reduced as well!

There were some further unrelated benefits of this daily inventory control. Instead of an ad hoc placing of orders for bulk chemicals, placed when the inventory manager saw the sight glass running low, end of day volumes of every chemical were now reported, and with daily volume sales being tallied, it was possible to forecast when supplies would need replenishing. Even better, it was possible to calculate very early on what annual consumption of each chemical would be and negotiate volume discounts up front, subject to subsequent audit. These volume discounts gave us another three to five percent margin improvement!

You don't have to be in a bulk distribution business for gross margin analysis to be a valuable tool. It can be applied to all types of project management.

Way Points Measure Performance

For example, in a professional services firm which provides consulting services to international clients, a "cost plus" methodology consisting of billable hours plus travel expenses, is the most easily understood and most frequently used method of setting price. A well managed consulting practice would actually prefer a fixed fee for the job, as the ability to complete the work in a very short time leads to a significantly greater profit than billing at standard hourly rates would do. And a cynical client should prefer a fixed fee to protect himself against a lazy consultant working slowly because he doesn't have another job to go to when this one finishes!

Assuming that we are able to persuade our clients that a fixed fee is the best way to go, how do we determine internally whether or not we have made a "profit" on the job, and how can we use numerical metrics to attempt to grade our own project managers' performance?

The answer is through a gross margin analysis by contract—which also serves the dual purpose of being the project task management worksheet or job control sheet. The project should have defined "waypoints" just like an airplane flight. By verifying the time it has taken to get to each waypoint, in terms of person hours, a good estimate can be made concerning whether completion of the project, equivalent to the pilot landing, will be reached on schedule.

The job control sheet comprises the following data points:

- Subsets of the project, by person hours, budgeted and actual.

- Standard cost per billable hour. This should include all the direct employee costs—salary, benefits, employment taxes paid by the employer, training, and a percentage mark-up for holidays and paid vacation. In total, these costs will typically add another fifty percent to the employee's actual hourly salary which must be recouped from each hour actually "worked" as billable time.

Notice that this cost does not include any costs associated with office overhead. This is because we are performing a gross margin analysis. A separate financial analysis should have been performed to identify what gross margin is needed from each consultant in order to cover the other costs of selling, management, administrative support, etc.

Used as a weekly management tool, these analyses will ensure that the waypoints are met on schedule and that the job is delivered profitably, as any course deviation will be noticed almost immediately and corrective action can be taken!

Conclusion

The fraud discovered by margin analysis is further proof that the numbers tell the story! And by understanding the story, you can MAKE THE NUMBERS HAPPEN!

CHAPTER 11

Don't Be Taken for a Ride— Transportation Costs

If It Flies or Floats, It's Cheaper to Rent It!

Planes are expensive to operate. It is often stated as a rule of thumb that the operating costs of a plane are four times the fuel cost. That is approximately true! Obviously, if it were completely true, then any savings obtained from reducing consumption of AvGas would be multiplied four-fold. But we know that that is not entirely the case for planes because of the high fixed costs of depreciation, life limited parts, insurance, annual inspections, hangars, etc. Because of these high fixed costs, if you only use your plane or boat for fewer than about 100 hours per year, it provides support for the old joke among pilots and sailors that if it flies or floats, it's cheaper to rent it! Or the other joke, what are the two happiest days in a boat owner's life? The day he buys it and the day he sells it!

But back in the corporate world, renting being better than buying is not true of heavily used commercial vehicles, where careful management of owned assets can prove to be more than twice as cost effective as leasing. The key point to emphasize is "careful." And as we have discovered, the failure to take care of assets and lack of control in administrative functions is likely to go hand-in-hand. In badly managed companies, it is often visible by the shocking disregard of employees and managers for properly taking care of expensive plant and machinery.

In many ways it is surprising that senior managers would allow corporate assets to be abused. Logic would dictate that company vehicles should be maintained in top condition, not only for safety reasons, but also delivery reliability. And because a corporate vehicle is a moving billboard, its condition, and the way it is driven can significantly influence outside perceptions of the company for both good and bad by the members of the public. A dirty, damaged, pollution emitting vehicle being driven carelessly or aggressively can significantly dent your company's image.

It is well known that UPS, for example, requires its drivers to turn off the truck's engine every time a delivery is made (see Appendix 7). A clean, quiet vehicle parked with its engine off presents a positive image of a calm company in charge of its own destiny. But what does lack of pride of ownership tell employees about how management regards the company's assets?

Clearly, a focus on maintaining a clean and attractive fleet of vehicles driven carefully and conscientiously is an integral part of *The 12-Step Plan* to maximizing profitability.

How do we implement a mini-12-step plan for transportation management and what are the benefits? By focusing on the factors below, we will see immediate savings of 30 percent of transportation costs, and tangential benefits of further ingraining the new corporate philosophy of care and control. The total cost of ownership of operating a fleet of vehicles is dependent on the following factors:

- Capital Cost—The initial cost of the vehicle itself.

- Depreciation—How long it is kept.

- Accident Free—The driver's personal characteristics—
  a clean driving record.

- Fuel Consumption—The time it spends with its engine
  on—no idling, and how aggressively it is driven.

- Maintenance—The way it is driven—the driver's skills.

To minimize the total cost of ownership, we need to fully understand how all these integrate with one another and take action in the following twelve areas:

1. *Buy a vehicle, do not lease.*

    There are many good leasing companies around today, with aggressive pricing and excellent maintenance programs. However, no matter how keen the pricing, there is no getting away from the fact that a lease is nothing more than a medium term rental, and at the end of the day, the truck has to be returned to its owners, leaving you and your company with nothing. Sure, the headache of maintaining the vehicle was taken off your hands, but given that if you lease a vehicle, it is new, there should not be much maintenance to perform anyway!

    Leasing a vehicle always includes an element of profit for the leasing company, and will usually force replacement with another new vehicle after five years. A significant incentive to replace the vehicle is often built into leases by requiring uneconomic lease rates after the initial five year term is up, or by specifying up front an uncompetitive buyout price.

    The advantages of leasing, e.g. that financing is obtained without a bank or with poor credit, and that maintenance is taken care of, are not sufficient reasons, in my opinion, to outweigh the overall negative impact on profitability by leasing. By far, the most cost effective way to operate a truck fleet is to own the vehicles, and keep them for a very long time.

2. *Buy a two year old vehicle if possible.*

    Any vehicle that has miles on it costs less. Purchase one that is at least two years old. So doing will reduce the purchase price by 50 percent. An incidental benefit is that insurance premium will also drop commensurately.

3. *Keep the vehicle until the end of its useful life—150,000 miles or more.* If vehicles can be purchased two years old, and then kept for 150,000 miles or more, the depreciation charges per mile will be minimized, and maintenance and reliability will not have become operational issues. We'll see below how to reduce the amount of necessary maintenance!

    The book value of the vehicles will be close to zero after 100,000 miles so the cost of insurance, tax and finance will also be significantly reduced. Today's vehicle reliability is such that for properly maintained vehicles, 150,000 miles is not unreasonable.

4. *Maintain pride of ownership.*

    In an ideal world, a specific truck will be allocated to a specific driver, and that driver will be held responsible for taking care of the truck. All vehicles will require periodic maintenance, but aggressive drivers whose vehicles need more frequent brake replacements, or other "unscheduled" services need to be made aware of this and their performance reviews annotated to negatively reflect their lack of concern for the company's property.

    The first step to keeping the vehicles running smoothly and with minimal maintenance is to offer both carrots and sticks to the drivers to treat the vehicles with care. Allocating a specific vehicle to a specific driver as much as possible, and then allowing that driver to purchase the vehicle at below blue book value when it is time to sell is a great motivator!

Create a corporate policy that sells the vehicle to its driver at the end of its useful life with the company. If the driver knows he will be able to purchase it for a bargain price, he will have a personal incentive to look after it while it is in the company's possession.

5. *Perform driver background checks.*

Do not hire anyone who has been convicted of DUI into any position which requires driving company vehicles or regularly driving rental vehicles on company business. Ensure that company policy requires that for any employee required to drive on business, a DUI is a firing offense. A DUI on a driver's record will double the insurance premium, and as a corporate executive, do you want to run the risk of an irresponsible employee causing an accident which kills an innocent bystander? In some jurisdictions, knowingly allowing a driver with a DUI conviction to operate a corporate vehicle could lead to personal liability in the event of an accident.

Insurance rates charged to the company (and accidents) will come down by having zero tolerance for DUIs in those positions. There is a reason that the FAA is notified by a State's Motor Vehicle Department if a pilot is issued a DUI while driving. The FAA will revoke the pilot's license. The FAA has found a clear relationship between DUI and accidents—so as a private company, let's take advantage of their many years and millions of dollars of research so that we too can avoid expensive errors.

6. *Create an "Acceptable Driving Standards" Policy.*

Specify what are acceptable driving standards and what will ensure drivers are trained in understanding them. Examples include no aggressive driving, such as speeding, racing up to red traffic lights, tailgating, or weaving. Aggressive acceleration wastes gas. Unnecessary braking caused by not looking more than the car ahead wears out brakes rapidly. Smooth driving, on the other hand, extends transmission life, saves on gas and other maintenance costs.

7. *Install GPS Systems.*

    Installing a GPS and letting drivers know about it provides not only information about abuse of corporate property, but also provides a defense in the event a driver is involved in an accident which is not his fault. Knowing where a vehicle is at all times prevents personal use and can assist in scheduling additional stops after a delivery vehicle has been dispatched. Advanced GPS systems can also be tied to invoicing systems, and maintenance tracking.

    It is possible today to track vehicles for less than $50 per month. This is a small price to pay for the "care" effect caused by employees knowing their driving habits are being monitored.

8. *Define Aggressive Driving and Make Accidents Firing Offenses.*

    I do not subscribe to the widely held view that traffic accidents are random events which will statistically happen to everyone. I believe that 90 percent of accidents can be avoided by defensive driving. This means actively looking out for the other idiots and taking evasive action when you see them do what you anticipated they would do, even if you have the right of way. Most freeway merge accidents happen because the person with "the right of way" on the highway failed to yield to an inconsiderate driver coming from the on-ramp. Most parking lot accidents happen because someone driving down an alleyway doesn't yield to the careless person reversing out of a space without looking. Yes, it is frustrating to have to always compensate for others' lack of ability, but is being right worth the time wasted in filling out a police report if you do decide to maintain your "right of way?"

In flying, as in driving, there are rules governing right of way. In fact, rules from the FAA govern every aspect of flight. But there is one paragraph which is my favorite. In layman's terms it says:

"If in the opinion of the pilot, in the interests of safety,
you need to break one of these rules, you may do so,"

… provided that you file a report with the FAA explaining why you did so. All good pilots when flying, will, if necessary to avoid an emergency, break the rules, and then deal with the paperwork to the FAA when they get on the ground. Filing a government report is far more preferable than your estate arranging a funeral, (although with the amount of paperwork the FAA requires, maybe only marginally so!).

Back on the ground in your corporate truck, in order to avoid accidents, a similarity exists—in that it is better to let the other

person break the rules, while you take evasive action, than to run into them and then deal with paperwork explaining why they were at fault. Irrespective of legal liability, if you could have taken evasive action, you are far better off doing so.

To ingrain this attitude into drivers' minds you have to take the carrot and stick approach here as well—the carrot being that they will be trained on defensive driving courses and perhaps even receive a bonus for an accident free year. The stick is that they will be fired if they are legally liable for causing an accident. This last statement which may be perceived as harsh, especially by the affected driver, is necessary for the survival of the company in terms of its vehicle liability insurance rates. Companies which have accident free records might pay one quarter of the liability rates as do companies where accidents are tolerated. And in terms of conscience, is it better to relieve a bad driver from his duties, or tolerate an employee who may injure or kill an innocent private citizen by his actions?

9. *Proper Route Planning, and Route Planning Software*
   In three of the TurnArounds I have been involved with, transportation has played a significant role in the business and been a large proportion of total costs. All of the above suggestions can be implemented without any significant investment in new systems. And even route planning can begin without a software system.

   Below are four real life examples of how to save on delivery costs before you even begin using a software-based system.

   a. Do not double up on routes. If you have "technicians" making service calls and "drivers" making deliveries to the same customer, it is far more cost effective to have the technicians make the deliveries at the same time as they make their service calls.

b. Do not drive past customers on the way to another delivery. If necessary, extend a route. One of my clients made weekly deliveries from a central location which required on one day driving two hours to a city, spending four hours delivering in that city, and then returning to base. The following day, they drove through that city and spent another four hours delivering further away. When we combined the route into one 12 hour route, the wage cost, even at time and a half for the overtime part, was reduced by 12.5 percent and the vehicle operating costs by 25 percent.

c. There are many situations where four 10-hour days are more cost-effective than five 8-hour days. Avoidance of rush hours is one benefit. Being able to recruit employees who like working a four day week for a five day wage is another. If routes cover large geographic areas, (as in b, above), it may be possible to accomplish in four 10-hour days what might otherwise require six 8-hour days.

d. If your company fleet is limited, do not schedule all manufactured products to leave your factory on the 32nd or 33rd of the month, (yes I have seen a month's books kept open to account for late deliveries). This requires third party transport solutions those few last days, while your own trucks sit idle for the first four weeks of the month. Schedule manufacturing appropriately for deliveries throughout the month to level load the truck fleet.

Once you have understood the basics of route planning, and have introduced the major efficiencies to be accomplished by planning and thinking about how to serve your customers, the final savings can be obtained by introducing route planning software.

There are many good packages on the market which take into account time of day, interstate vs. side roads, etc. They can also link to real time GPS tracking, keeping track of scheduled mainte-nance, and even invoicing from locations. Determine what is best for you and then send out an RFP to software vendors. But remem-ber the first rule of computer programming—garbage in, garbage out. If your fleet management staff does not run a smooth operation without a computer system, they must be brought up to speed before the software is.

10. *Eliminate left turns.*

The UPS Approach to Fuel Saving—No Left Turns

UPS, one of the biggest consumers of diesel fuel in the US, deter-mined it could save three million gallons of fuel every year by reducing the number of left turns it makes. Left turns usually require at least one cycle of a traffic light, averaging two minutes of engine idle. In addition, UPS demands that their drivers turn off their engines for every package stop. Route Management Software enables them to put various criteria into the parameters and as a result, they are minimizing their costs. UPS claims that they have reduced costs by six percent because of the time saved and reduced fuel burn by planning routes to minimize the number of left turns. Walmart is now following suit.

The environmental movement could learn a lot from these corporations if they truly wanted to "save the planet." Rather than mandating what the car companies produce in terms of mandating ever stiffer CAFE standards, the environmentalists should focus on educating the public to change their driving habits and emulate the examples of UPS and Wal-Mart. This would do more to reduce emissions than any amount of tinkering with CAFE standards!

11. *Introduce a Corporate-wide Gas Card.*

In our capacity of Private Pilot, back at the airport, we would never dream of climbing into our plane, turning on the engine, and then figuring out where to go. The hourly costs of operating aircraft engines are just too high to allow idle time. But I have seen truck drivers "clock-in" at 6 a.m., go to their truck and start it up, and then go to the company cafeteria for breakfast, or to the break room to read a newspaper, while they wait for their day's instructions. Not only is this environmentally unfriendly, it has doubled the fuel costs of operating these trucks. So the first rule of fleet management is: *Don't start the vehicle until you are ready to go!*

In order to be able to identify profligate users of fuel, each driver should be issued with a corporate fuel card which requires drivers to enter current odometer reading every time they fill up. Ensure that monthly statements are reconciled to the actual mileage of the truck. Calculate the average miles per gallon obtained by each driver and truck. This will enable you to spot anomalies such as filling up personal vehicles using the corporate card, or observing that a vehicle's fuel consumption is significantly worse than EPA estimates or compared with others in the fleet. Do not allow excessive warm up and require engines to be turned off when vehicle is stopped. Today's diesel engines do not require continuous running.

Fuel usage is often the best place to start attempting to save money on transportation costs. Fuel can be saved in many areas, most of which require behavioral changes, and as managers, we are paid to implement those behavioral changes. The MBA financial analyst can judge how to reduce the number of actual miles driven, but, without changing our employees' behaviors before, during and after the journey, we will not improve our efficiency per mile.

12. *Maximize Insurance Deductibles.*

With all of the above measures in place, you will have a fleet of safe drivers and accidents will be a rarity. Take advantage of this and only insure for the major risks.

Insurance costs can be steep, but ratings are based on a number of factors, including the vehicle itself, the driver and company policies toward driving. If the vehicle is valuable, the highest possible deductible should be accepted for liability—with the company "self insuring" the amount of the deductible. If the company doesn't want the unpredictable fluctuation in expense which might occur if an accident happens, the amount of insurance premium savings from moving to a high deductible can be charged in the P+L to "insurance expense" and the money physically transferred to a reserve account. If the vehicle is of little value, it may not even be worth insuring for more than third party liability.

Conclusion

Just as in aircraft flight planning, where the route is chosen to minimize total operational as well as flying time, you should look at all the variables associated with running a truck fleet.

By driver training, pride of ownership, route management, and setting expectations, vehicle fleet costs can be reduced by 30 percent.

CHAPTER 12

Taxes

Free Money Is Yours for the Asking

It is said that starting the engine of your plane is like setting hundred dollar bills on fire. The difference is that you actually get to hear your bills burn when the plane engine is turned on and *AvGas* smells good! That throaty roar when you accelerate down the runway is a far bigger adrenaline rush than anything that could be obtained from burning hundred dollar bills.

Paying taxes can also be likened to burning hundred dollar bills—except that unlike the emotion you feel when you fire up a plane's engine, the only feeling you get when you send your check to the taxman is one of deep depression. But wouldn't it be great if you didn't have to send as much money? In fact, wouldn't it be a fun intellectual challenge between you and the taxman to be so conversant with common tax issues that you revisit your historical tax reporting to identify significant overpayments from prior years?

You might be asking why there is a chapter on taxes in a book about turning around unprofitable businesses. Surely, if a company is making a loss, it is not going to be paying taxes. Well, that might possibly be true about corporate income taxes, but that assumes that the book loss—what you report to your shareholders and the bank—is the same as the tax loss—what you report to the tax authorities. Because of tax incentives such as accelerated depreciation, it is often possible that a cash flow positive company pays no income tax, but a company which ceased investing in new fixed assets a few years ago may now be paying taxes from depreciation recapture, even though it is now operating at a loss.

This chapter goes into more than just income taxes. Income taxes are usually managed by the audit firm or tax CPA, after the results of the year are known. There are opportunities to be proactive during the year, such as concerning the timing of fixed asset additions, or segregating costs for the R+D tax credit, but in a company losing money, tax planning is likely to be close to last on the agenda of issues facing day-to-day managers.

What is more important is managing the day-to-day activities so that taxes on purchasing, sales, payroll, and fixed assets are minimized. And if you are a company which has gone through many rounds of share issuances, such as a venture capital funded company incorporated in Delaware, understanding how that state bills you for Franchise Tax and the alternative method available to you, could save you $180,000 annually!

Purchasing

Sales Taxes Paid
If you are located in an unincorporated county, but have a "city" postal address, or if your zip code covers two tax jurisdictions, then I will guarantee that your company will be overcharged on the sales tax rate by your new suppliers, and especially by your on-line suppliers.

With the multiplicity of taxes now being charged, and tax authorities aggressively seeking revenues from all sources, regular suppliers and sales tax software program vendors all want to ensure that they do not become liable for any underpayment of taxes as a result of their invoicing practices. Therefore, whenever there is a multiplicity of rates charged in a zip code, or to an unincorporated area which is assigned to a city by the US Postal Service, the vendor, by default, will charge you the highest possible rate it can find for your generic area, no matter what the specific tax rate for your street.

As a real world example, the metropolitan area of Denver, Colorado, is made up of many home rule cities, special districts, and unincorporated counties. In general, city and special district taxes will add about four percent to the overall sales tax rate charged by the state and county. If you are in an unincorporated part of Arapahoe, or Jefferson counties, to use two examples I am familiar with, you might have a postal address of Englewood or Littleton, both cities with high sales taxes.

If you are spending $10 million per year on manufacturing raw materials and office supplies, being over-charged at the city rate instead of the unincorporated county rate could add $400,000 to your cost of goods sold. Correcting this error could increase your operating profit margin by four percent without resorting to price increases or staff layoffs. Free money!

How do we solve this problem to receive this free money? With regular suppliers, an affidavit that you are in an unincorporated location usually suffices. If it doesn't, change suppliers. For on-line purchases, or other suppliers who swear by their sales tax program, providing them with your "zip+4" postal code usually works. In many cases, because there are so many tax jurisdictions, these software programs are continuing works in process and your input may be used to make the software program more accurate.

It is critical however, to remain vigilant, and ensure that in the purchase invoice approval process, not only are quantities and descriptions verified, but that the tax rate is stated correctly as well.

WARNING—for Shared Services Subscribers: I have found that multi-location companies who use shared services centers for invoice processing invariably pay more for their purchases than those who control expenditures at the factory level. The "ownership" issue is the main reason, but with one particular client I achieved a four percent cost reduction. The shared service center was so far away geographically that they did not understand the concept that a "postal" city's boundaries could be different from a rural tax jurisdiction's boundaries! So they simply ignored the incorrect tax rate being charged by most vendors.

Taxes due are a liability which can become a personal liability of directors. It is therefore critical that they are calculated correctly and paid when due. Ensure that all goods and services are appropriately invoiced and returns filed on a timely basis. In many jurisdictions in which the tax due might be minimal, late fees and penalties on failure to file might be many times the actual taxes due!

Payroll Taxes

Unless your staff numbers exceed 400, it is my recommendation that you use an outsourced payroll management company to process all of your payroll checks. While your in-house payroll clerk will probably complain about the time it takes to input the data to the outsourced system, and it is true that data has to be at the outside firm well in advance of payroll due date, the tax compliance matters taken care of by the payroll service more than make up for the slight inconvenience that their data reporting might require.

And, if you have undertaken the recommendations of Chapter 4, *Zero Tolerance for Error*, and banned overtime, the payroll hours paid will not vary from week to week anyway!

What taxes are due on payroll and what reports need to be filed? And how can there be free money here? Besides the Federal 940s and 941s, whose filing frequency and timing will depend on gross value of payroll—the higher your payroll, the more frequently you need to file—you will need to file tax reports in every state in which you do business, and in some cities as well. Denver, for example, has a Head Tax, which the City Council euphemistically calls an "Occupational Privilege Tax." If your company is based in Ohio, but you have a salesman resident in Denver, you will have to file a report with the OPT to Denver. I'm sure you will agree that outsourcing your payroll to a national firm who knows what needs to be filed by location is far easier than paying one of your accounting staff to search the Internet for every possible tax due on every employee based on the address of their homes!

Typically, states require quarterly and annual payroll tax filings. For a continuing business, e.g. your headquarters or manufacturing facility, that is relatively easy—you will be a continuing business and the only thing that will change quarter-to-quarter is gross payroll. However, if you have remote employees—typically salesmen—who change, it is highly likely that a replacement regional salesman with an eight state territory will not reside in the same state as the salesman he replaces. For reporting purposes, this requires filing "final" reports in the state in which the outgoing salesman lived, and "new company" reports in the state in which the new salesman resides.

It is absolutely critical that when you file a "final" state report, you send the report by certified mail, and keep copies of the reports for at least seven years. It would be wise to keep copies of the employee's termination papers with the reports as well. This is because as states get hungrier for tax receipts, they will dig further and further back in their archives to find "errors." Yet it is my belief, having seen too many of these "requests for back tax," that states are trying to resurrect old issues in the hope that the corporations they are seeking funds from can no longer find their old records and feel that it is a more efficient business decision to pay the few thousand dollars demanded than defend themselves. Most of the cases I have seen have sought $2,000 to $4,000 in back taxes. The largest demand I saw from a state was for $18,000. The original demand letter stated that the adjustment was as a result of a Federal Audit seven years before. When we presented the state with the Federal "No Change" notice (meaning that the audit had failed to

For some reason FREE MONEY seems lighter...

uncover any additional taxes being due), the state then came back and claimed that we had failed to file the tax return for the year in question seven years ago.

When we mentioned to them the statute of limitations, they claimed that there was no statute of limitations on "failure to file." Fortunately, we had copies of our return, the check for original taxes paid, and a post office receipt for certified mail. However, without good archiving, we could easily have been on the hook for $18,000. This would have been the least of the costs we would have had to bear, because once the tax authorities have found an error in your tax accounting, you have a tarnished reputation and they will hound you for many more years to come.

Business Personal Property Taxes—the Taxes on Fixed Assets

Presently, my home base is Colorado, and I considered heading this section "Why Colorado Chases Away all Manufacturing Industries." That is because Colorado has the fourth highest Business Personal Property Tax in the country. (* Report of Colorado Legislative Staff, Aug 19, 2004). However, as 41 states charge business personal property tax, this section of the book may enable you to slash those taxes by 50 percent. This is because personal property taxes, for which a bill is generally sent automatically every spring, is usually assumed to be correct, is always budgeted for, and because it is "government," is felt to be non-negotiable. These assumptions are wrong! By spending time to correct the inaccuracies in this billing, usually of your own making, you will obtain refunds and pay less in the future. This is the best kind of money—it is free—and its margins are infinite!

Why do I assert with confidence that there is free money for the asking? Because most companies' fixed asset ledgers significantly overstate the number of assets the company owns. I am NOT saying that the total values of all the assets owned are incorrect in the financial statements—far from it. But because of high depreciation rates, the net book value of old assets is probably close to zero, and when those assets are disposed of, no one bothers to think about taking them off the fixed asset ledger because they have no value anyway.

Every year, if you are in one of the business personal property tax states, the state, through your local county, requires a personal property tax declaration of all fixed assets used in your business. The form is relatively simple. It asks for a list of all assets added, and all assets disposed of. The form, like all tax forms, is subject to audit, and there are stiff penalties for false declarations.

Consequently, most law abiding CFOs complete the form by providing a list of all assets added during the year—because they usually have good records of what was added. After all, they had to write a check to obtain them! What they usually don't have, is a list of those assets they got rid of. Because most of the things they got rid of were valueless, they were either thrown away, given away or lost.

In general, the CFO doesn't care about tracking disposals, because the asset was old and probably was fully depreciated i.e. had no financial value to the company. So if an auditor were to do a test of asset values, he would look for high value assets on the ledger and verify they existed on the company's premises. He would not be looking for zero book value assets.

The tax problem however, is that even though the old assets have no monetary value to the company, to a county property tax assessor, everything has a value, and in Colorado, the minimum value to which something can be depreciated to for tax purposes is 18 percent of its original cost.

I had one client whose fixed asset ledger at the time of my engagement showed assets with a gross original cost of $15 million. They had accumulated $13 million of depreciation, for a net book value of $2 million. From my "management by wandering around" I knew that the actual cost of assets in place was well below $15 million, in fact probably less than half that. So I asked the purchasing manager to undertake a project to identify all of the assets that the company still owned. By the time the project was complete, she had found that the net book value was about right—we did have assets worth about $2 million, but that was made up of a gross cost of $5 million with accumulated depreciation of $3 million. The other $10 million of fully depreciated assets (primarily a large mainframe computer system) had been disposed of many years ago, but never removed from the fixed asset ledger.

Showing the new fixed asset ledger to the property tax auditor resulted (after many discussions) in a refund of $500,000 in overpaid prior taxes, and an ongoing annual reduction of tax to be paid of well into six figures. For a two month project, this was an incredible rate of return!

Business personal property taxes are one of the most onerous taxes a business faces. They are a tax on doing business. They have to be paid whether you make money or not. They have to be paid whether you use the asset or not. And if you are a manufacturing business suffering through a significant downturn, where 75 percent of your assets are mothballed, they could by themselves cause your business to fail.

Unlike Real Estate taxes, which are due on the appraised value of your land and buildings, business personal property taxes are calculated on the original cost of all of the machines, appurtenances, and office equipment you use to go about your daily business. They are not quite as insidious as inventory taxes, but almost so. Different states use different methods to value assets, but the reason you are likely to be paying twice as much in personal property taxes as you really should be is your own fault!

Franchise Taxes in Delaware

No matter where you are physically located, there is a high likelihood that your state of incorporation is Delaware. This is primarily because Delaware Corporate Law is very favorable to directors and investors in terms of limiting personal liability. Because of this attraction to companies, the state of Delaware is the second highest in the country, after Alaska, in its taxation of "miscellaneous" items i.e., NOT income, sales or property.

And what it charges you, my dear non-Delaware located business, is called a Franchise Tax. The State calculates this tax based on one of two alternatives—the "Authorized Share Method," or the "Assumed Par Value Method." These methods provide startlingly different tax bills, and you may rest assured that the state will send you the bill using the method which is most favorable to it—usually the Authorized Share Method.

If you are a typical start-up company with grand visions of becoming the next Google, you probably have an authorized share issuance capacity of 25 million shares. But you may have only issued 2 million of them to date, and may only have gross assets of $25 million.

Under the Authorized Share method, the first bill you will receive from the State of Delaware will ask for $180,000. But if you obtain the forms for calculating your liability under the Assumed Par Value method, you will be able to send them a check for $8,750 and be all square!

So if your new CFO finds that you have been paying under the Authorized Share Method in the past, he's just earned his first few months' salary!

Information on how to accomplish this saving can be found at *corp.delaware.gov/taxcalc.shtml.*

Conclusion

In terms of maximizing corporate profitability, the tax savings identified above reduced "sundry" taxes paid by 75 percent, and represented an increase in gross margin of three percent for my client. A reasonable pre income tax gross profit margin for a company is ten percent. A company can effectively raise its profits by a third, simply by paying attention to sundry taxes and keeping pristine accounting records. It is an exceptional use of corporate resources, and demonstrates again why having in your CFO first and foremost a businessman, who just happens to be a good accountant, will pay dividends an order of magnitude greater than the incumbent's salary.

Now that you know where to find the free money and how to claim it, let's go set some of those $100 bills on fire and turn some *AvGas* into noise!

CHAPTER 13

How to Maximize International Profitability

The Principles Are the Same, the Rules May Be different

"Emergency at 33,000 Feet"

We were at 33,000 feet above eastern Canada and I had just settled into watching the movie, *Swing Vote*, starring Kevin Costner. The movie is a spoof on what politicians will do and say to get themselves elected. Or is there possibly more truth behind it than we would care to believe? Interrupting the entertainment, the Captain announced that for the benefit of those who had not been watching the moving map screen at the front of the cabin that we had turned around and would be returning to Chicago. There was nothing to worry about, he breezed calmly, as they all do; he had just noticed an over-temperature indicator in one of the engines and it was now operating at idle thrust. Translation: "I've shut down an engine because it was on fire."

The plane became silent and I looked at the in-flight route and information screen, because, as a pilot myself, I wanted to understand what was going on. He concluded his announcement in the standard no-stress drawl that most long-haul pilots have perfected with the usual, "So just sit back and relax and if anything changes, I'll be sure to let you know."

About two minutes later, the plane's nose dropped precipitously, and everything began to shake violently as we began an emergency descent at 6,000 feet per minute. A slightly less relaxed pilot commanded the cabin crew to "prepare the aircraft for immediate landing, we will be on the ground in Toronto in six minutes."

My brain sped through the mental calculations about how much fuel had been burned so far and I realized that we were still over MLW (maximum landing weight) and would need to land 30 knots faster than normal on one engine. The last plane which had overshot a runway at Toronto was an Air France A340 which had subsequently caught fire, in August 2005. With that fact in mind, I fervently hoped that our Captain would command all his ingrained knowledge from multiple training exercises of landing the plane gently on the numbers. This is because he would need to avoid a landing gear collapse, and, with only one engine operating, he would not have the benefit of reverse thrust to help stop us before the ravine which had entrapped the Air France flight.

Suffice it to say, the landing was perfect, the fire engines weren't needed, and the only problem was a people issue because as it was after midnight, all the customs officials had gone home and we needed to be officially processed to "enter Canada." When will governments recognize that the risk of a passenger jumping ship and illegally entering Canada is not likely to happen as a result of an engine catching fire? Requiring dazed passengers to line up single file for three hours to be processed by the most junior official they could wake up in the middle of the night is unlikely to lead to an increase in future tourism!

"Expecting the Unexpected"

So how does successfully landing a 777 on one engine in Canada relate to improving the international profitability of American firms? Answer—very closely.

The first thing to recognize about managing an international subsidiary from the US is that it is not located "just around the corner." It is therefore difficult to get to. Unless you live on the east coast of the US and are only going to England, you will be required to take an overnight flight. Unless you live in a major US city, you will be required to make a connection to a flight at an international gateway. The departures of these flights are invariably delayed as cross country connecting flights coming from snow bound or thunderstorm affected airports in the mid-west are late inbound. Because the connecting flight always seems to have two first class passengers aboard who will be joining your flight to Europe, you will wait! So, as the Boy Scout motto implores, "Be prepared."

If nothing else, on an international trip, assume something WILL go wrong, and if it doesn't, then that is a bonus. Such anticipation of the unexpected means at its most basic, you will plan to arrive at your destination at least a day ahead of your first important meeting. Not only will this mean you are not stressed by any operational problems, it gives you a chance to truly freshen up (are arrivals lounges with showers really sufficient?), and see a bit of the local area so that you can show interest in and knowledge of the foreign culture you are visiting to the people you are meeting with. When my plane to Europe caught fire, it was no big deal, (at least after we had landed safely), as I had left Denver on a Friday afternoon, expecting to arrive in Copenhagen on Saturday afternoon in time for a meeting on Monday morning. All that was ruined by my arriving in Copenhagen late on Sunday morning was a half day of sightseeing! My meetings took place as scheduled.

For the pilots of the 777, their training of "expect a problem" usually means engine failure. Therefore, when the actual event happens, they themselves go into personal "autopilot" and take care of the problem without a fuss. If your training for an overseas trip is also to "expect a problem" then you will have brought more than 24 hours of reading materials and music to listen to. This is particularly wise if you too are diverted to a deserted airport in the middle of the night and have to wait for a back-up plane and crew to arrive. And when our new plane finally arrived, it proved the airline policies of seniority! Most junior airline staff members get the worst job, sitting around an airport on "reserve," while the most senior secure the cushy international flights which allow them to complete their monthly allotment of 72 hours flying in about four trips! The new cabin crew's average age was probably 30 years younger than the one they replaced! They were fired up and ready to go!

The reactions of the pilots, to the real emergency, and of me, to the unexpected 20 hour delay—both of calm, taken in stride—reinforced the idea that the most important criterion in "The 12-Step Plan to Successful Turnarounds" is planning. Proper planning ensures a successful outcome for a business or for a flight.

Business Class for Half the Price

What additional planning steps should be part of the preparation for an overseas journey in order to not only make it effective, but also "cost-effective?" How can the travel costs be minimized without compromising comfort and convenience? First of all, on a long trip, I think that the advantages of flying business class are worth a few thousand dollars. However, I do not think they are worth the $8,000 additional typically quoted as an upgrade from *pleb class*. (That is the name Sir Richard Branson once considered calling Virgin Airlines' Economy Class—the opposite of the British "Upper Class" which is his first class cabin). But with proper planning, it is almost always possible to fly to Europe, business class, on a major US airline, for less than $4,000, round-trip. This is because while the airlines don't aggressively advertise this possibility, and some travel agents would prefer to earn their overrides by selling expensive tickets, the vast majority of US travelers to overseas destinations simply do not expect to see the APEX or "advance purchase = low fares" concept, to apply to business class tickets. The biggest reason for not snagging these low cost business class tickets is entirely within your control.

I have witnessed too many executives who wait until the last minute to finalize plans. Why? You are the executive. Are you not in control of your destiny? To minimize your costs and maximize your effectiveness, your schedule should be planned sufficiently far in advance that you are fully prepared for all of your meetings. If you know that you typically have a few cancellations on a trip, then consider over-scheduling to begin with. Finally, given that even when you are out of the office, the emails and phone calls never end, in the unlikely event that a meeting you scheduled three weeks ago unexpectedly gets cancelled the week before your trip, you will not be twiddling your thumbs!

Also, if you are new to dealing with executives in Europe and Asia, please be aware that the business culture truly is different from that in the US. Cancellations of appointments "penciled in" are an American thing. It may be more difficult to set up an appointment overseas than in the US, but in general, Europeans, Latin Americans and Asians will honor appointments once made. So the most likely person to cancel a meeting is you!

Once we have the dates set we want to snag that $4,000 ticket. If the airline doesn't offer a $4,000 round trip ticket to the city we specifically want to go to, how can we still manage to get where we want for the price we want? In most cases, one way mileage upgrades are available for 25,000 or 30,000 miles, and most airlines offer the opportunity to purchase miles for about three cents per mile. Even with the co-payments (which can now reach $500 for a one way upgrade award), added to the cost of purchasing a tourist class ticket, this method of traveling in business class still equates to a $4,000 round trip. And even if you are unable to guarantee that upgrade at the time of booking there is still a very high probability that a seat will be available on the day of flight. I can recall only one occasion where I was unable to upgrade using miles on the actual day of my flight, even though at the time of original booking I was waitlisted. So this method works!

A frequent explanation I have heard for executives insisting on buying full priced business class tickets is because of the flexibility they offer. This argument is specious. This flexibility is there, but even assuming that you need to change plans on one leg of your flight, you are still better off buying a $4,000 round trip ticket, and paying the $250 or $500 change fee for the return than buying a fully flexible ticket at the start.

Another interesting product of the airlines' yield management system is that they are able to take advantage of laziness or ignorance of travelers. Most European subsidiaries of American businesses are close to the major airline hubs of London, Paris and Frankfurt. US airlines know this. They therefore price those cities at premiums to regional cities, many of which also have direct service from the US by the same airline. So if your final destination is London or Frankfurt, you should consider traveling to Manchester or Dusseldorf and driving the rest of the way. As previously discussed in Chapter 6, *Travel and Entertainment—Yes!* The total journey time will still be about the same. And with the proliferation of low cost airlines within Europe, even if your final destination is a different capital city, it is usually possible to fly business class to a provincial city such as Manchester, UK, for less than $4,000 round trip, and there transfer to *Easyjet, FlyBe, SAS, AirBerlin* and others for the final hour of your journey.

"Where's the Beef?"

So far, you might be regarding the above as small potatoes in the grand scheme of things, but assume that in your company you have three executives who each travel six times per year overseas. Using these advance planning tips could save upwards of $100,000 annually, enough to pay the salary of an International Controller, who can spend time increasing your profits still more by his knowledge of the challenges you will encounter below. And solving these challenges can save you tens of millions of dollars!

Fly to a regional city or use miles to upgrade and travel to Europe half price!

The Legal Structure—Branch vs. Subsidiary

In one of my early successful TurnArounds, the client company had established a presence in Europe five years earlier. This was the first time the company had ventured abroad, and apart from the VP of International Operations, none of the senior executives, including the previous CFO, had had any international experience. Consequently, each of the local offices in Europe had been set up as a separate subsidiary company of the US Corporation. In France this meant a *Societe Anonyme* (SA) and in Germany a *GmbH*. By so doing, all of the assets, liabilities, tax loss carryforwards, or profits relating to each country, were trapped in each subsidiary. It was not possible to combine operations and allow one's profits to offset the other's losses.

Five years after initial establishment, European operations overall were slightly profitable, on a pre-tax basis, but losing more than $3 million per year after tax. "How could this be?" asked the CEO. The reason was because while Germany was making $5 million per year in profits, it was paying more than 60 percent in German income tax on those profits, yet France, the perennial loss maker, was getting no tax benefit within France from their substantial losses. And because each company was a separate legal entity within its own country, the profits and losses were not aggregated. Each country's tax authority treated its company on a stand-alone basis. To solve the loss making problem, to an outside observer, it would have been easy to say "shut down France" but for strategic reasons, France was deemed necessary to overall European success. Therefore, the task fell to me to find an out-of-the-box solution to turn this combined $3 million loss around.

After spending time studying French and German corporate and tax law, it appeared that an option would be to roll the French operation into a "branch" of Germany. And because it was the German

management within this company which had aggressively defended maintaining a French operation in order to preserve their own sales within Germany, we had a business reason for creating the branch. I therefore approached our outside audit firm to obtain a tax opinion on whether this would be possible. After much huffing and puffing and stating that this was "very unusual," the auditors agreed that it would be legal, and set about creating the paperwork.

Shortly thereafter, we transferred the business of the French subsidiary, "SA," into the company's French "GmbH." And at the next dinner I had with my French audit partner, he told me with pride how he had advised another American client to do the same—"and they were very 'appy." I never had the gall to ask him how much of a fee he had charged them for this advice!

Consider opening an overseas Branch rather than a Subsidiary.

Tax Me Once, Shame on You, Tax Me Twice, Shame on Me!

How can you be taxed on the same profit twice? Or, on some income, not at all? After all, in the US, a tax year ends on one day and a new tax year begins on the day after. So how could it be possible for one day to fall into two tax years? Or, for a day to be exempt from a tax year? This is the typical reaction of the typical American CFO who has been brought up under the "logical" American tax code.

Yet in some countries in Europe, because tax is NOT LOGICAL, and in some cases is based on cash rather than accrual basis of accounting, it is possible, when starting or ending the lives of companies, for some periods to either be taxed twice or not at all. The knowledge that this vagary in the law exists, is one of many reasons why there is significant value to a company with significant international operations, hiring as a CFO, someone who has had substantial international financial experience. Understanding how basic tax law can be significantly different across borders can be worth millions of dollars to the company.

This value was brought home spectacularly to my client when we restructured the French and German operations.

Not only did we have regular corporate income taxes to consider, we had VAT on sales and purchases, accrued liabilities, and recognition of gain on forgiveness of debt. And each was subject to a separate but interrelated tax regime.

We had originally planned on making the restructuring change at calendar year end, as the facilities would be closed anyway for a two week Christmas shutdown. The initial, logical, suggested date for the changeover, was December 31, but when I researched the potential impact of the date on the double-or-nothing taxing periods for all the different associated taxes, I was astounded to find that by doing a two-step reorganization, with one entity being closed down before Christmas, the intermediate entity having a life of about two weeks—and the new branch starting up on January 6, we were able to utilize many of the losses which would have evaporated if we had simply made the change on December 31. The tax savings as a result were in the millions of dollars.

Never be afraid of asking the seemingly stupid questions. Asking if there are tax consequences of changing a date for a reorganization might sound silly, if you have only worked under the US Tax Code, but in Europe, it is only to be expected!

Can Tax Loss Carryforwards Offset Profits?
Not in Germany Unless You Push

At the time I was working in Germany, our US parent had established a presence five years previously. Because of the large size of the operation, we had incurred losses in the first four years of our operations, (in two of those years we had lost money on a world-wide basis) but finally in year five, profits in Germany were flowing as freely as the beer in a Munich tent at Oktoberfest.

So when it was time to prepare the tax return, I was very happy to offset most of year five's profits with the accumulated tax loss carryforwards. After having delivered the return on time, and with appropriate funds, I was shocked to receive shortly thereafter, a demand for unpaid taxes on the remainder of the profits for the fifth year.

German tax law was clear. At that time, we were allowed to carry forward losses for seven years (we had done five). So I challenged the authorities to explain why they were ignoring this rule. Their response was typical of the xenophobia exhibited by the majority of local officials to foreign corporations worldwide. Please attempt to imagine the German accent in what follows when I describe the reaction at Tax HQ in Dusseldorf when I appeared with my copy of the German Tax Code, and my translator. For dramatic effect, the conversation below is abbreviated and not verbatim!

Me: "Clearly it states under code section blah, blah, blah, that tax losses can be carried forward for seven years and we only had five years of losses."

German tax men: "Jahrwohl, but zat is not zee intent of zee law."

Me: "I don't care about intent, I care about following the rules, something Germans are renowned for."

German tax men: "Zat ees gut, but in Germany, if you had been losing money for five years you vould haf closed down; zerefore, you vere creating fictitious intercompany invoices to artificially create a loss in Germany."

Me: "For two of those years, we lost money worldwide. And we are here for the long term."

German tax men: "Ve don't care—give us ze money."

Me: "No—we had a transfer pricing audit performed by the IRS in the US last year which identified that we had undercharged Germany, so in fact our losses in Germany should be greater which would mean that we are in fact owed a refund here!!!"

The upshot of this conversation was that the case progressed through higher and higher levels of German tax court, ultimately being settled in our favor at "Competent Authority" where representatives of the US IRS and Germany's Tax authorities resolve cases of international transfer pricing. The moral of the story is clear—if you are in the right, fight. Lack of knowledge often leads companies to settle, and the foreign tax jurisdictions will often play on this desire to settle … as will HR attorneys … as you will see in what follows!

Fight when you are right.

Pleasing the Office Instead of Pleasing the Customer

One morning, many years ago, I was sitting at my desk in Denver, making a few last minute preparations for my afternoon trip to London to announce a new organization chart and business strategy for my company's UK operations, when the phone rang.

A plummy upper class English accent announced itself as a solicitor (lawyer), verified who I was, and that I had authorized the termination of a young female sales rep in the London office the previous week. As she had been the only female, and we had retained the five male sales reps, he proceeded to demand a fee closely resembling the annual salary of the terminated account exec in lieu of a sex discrimination lawsuit.

As I was the one who had prepared the analysis determining who would go and who would stay in our UK office, I was very familiar with the numbers and this woman just hadn't been selling our product. I was later to find out what she had been selling, but right now, I was prepared to go to court to defend our decision. I was not going to settle simply because we were 5,000 miles away.

So I asked him if he would be in his office the following afternoon, and when he answered in the affirmative, I told him I would see him. Somewhat surprised he said, "You do realize I am in London don't you?" To which my response was "of course—for a matter this important, it is clearly necessary for us to talk face to face." He didn't need to know I had already planned to be there!

I met my Country Manager in London the following morning and proceeded to obtain affidavits from the staff that when the cat (Country Manager) was away, the mouse (this female sales rep) would play, and that the play involved some very bizarre behavior which one only expects in certain clubs. Armed with this information, I stunned the solicitor by declaring that based on my interviews with staff, I could provide a fairly detailed description of the various locations of this woman's body piercings. Suffice it to say that no further demands were made on the company.

The moral of this story is that frequently foreign attorneys will create sex, age, or race discrimination lawsuits against American companies simply because they know that the distance involved makes it difficult to protest a case, especially if one is going to be ultimately tried in front of a local jury. Therefore, any firing decisions MUST be made with the utmost respect for the local laws, in terms of notifying works councils in many parts of Europe, unions in most cases, regional employment offices, and other statutory bodies.

Also, it comes as a surprise to many American executives that after a probationary period, most European employees at all levels are provided with an employment contract which makes it very difficult to remove them. This includes management and sales staff, traditionally subject to "employment at will" in the US. In France and Belgium for example, great care should be taken when hiring sales staff, because according to local employment laws in place there, "A salesman does not have a duty to sell." If he is not making his quota, it is just as likely to be interpreted by an employment tribunal that your product's shortcomings are the problem, rather than his sales skills needing improvement!

Liability Insurance—What Liability?

As an American company abroad you want to protect your assets. And your large, US based insurer will be more than happy to insure every possible risk and liability, at American rates of premium. This is because the ultimate risk for an American company is to be sued in the US for a situation occurring overseas. However, in many cases, it can be expensive overkill, and the temptation to take such insurance should be avoided. Instead, if each foreign office is its own separate legal entity, primary insurance for that company should be placed in that country. In most cases, rates will be one half to one tenth of the rates charged by US based insurance companies for your foreign coverage.

This is because in the US, if someone is unhappy with your product, they will sue. If someone slides on the ice outside your office, they will sue. And in many cases, they will win. In Europe, they won't because they would be perceived as being careless and they would be laughed at. For example, the widespread response in Europe to the woman who spilled hot McDonald's coffee in her lap and won a multi-million dollar settlement from McDonalds was disbelief that her own carelessness could cause the purveyor to be held responsible for her accident.

As a result, US insurers feel it is their duty to protect you against any possible lawsuit. However, it pays to find out what local limits of liability might be. As an example, one of my clients had a Swedish office with 20 or so drivers of company cars. Our US insurance broker saw this as a significant risk and had insured each one for liabilities of $5 million, at a cost of about $2,000 per car. Yet when I went to Sweden to review this policy with the local Controller, I discovered that at that time, Swedish law restricted compensation to victims of road accidents to $60,000 per person! So we placed the liability insurance with a Swedish firm and reduced the premium costs by about $40k.

Local Country Audits and Filings—Why Bother?

While a financial audit is usually a necessary and valuable exercise in third party review of a subsidiary's operations, a statutory filing of local country accounts is frequently not needed. But many local auditors will not advise you that that is the case, or they might suggest to you that while it may not be legally necessary, it is advisable.

This frequently is the case in Europe where there are "small" and "medium" size company exemptions from filing requirements.

If your company can take advantage of these exemptions, why bother with going through a full blown audit, using a much smaller materiality level than you would need if simply preparing a US consolidated set of accounts? If the cost of each local country filing is $30,000, not filing when you don't have to soon adds up to dollars flowing to the bottom line!

Do You Really Need to Be in the Capital City?

For many US companies setting up foreign operations, there is a certain cachet to being in London or Paris. But unless you are in financial services, do you really need to be in London to serve the UK? No! With exceptional road, high speed rail, and domestic air services, nowhere in the UK is really more than 4 hours from anywhere else. But London real estate costs can be 10 times those in the provinces, and wages can be three times greater. Proximity to the customer is paramount, but if your UK office is serving Europe, for example, why not set up near one of the regional airports with a low cost carrier as its hub tenant?

In many of the regions throughout Europe, very significant tax incentives are offered by the governments for setting up businesses and decentralizing jobs away from the capital cities. Sometimes these subsidies may be equivalent to a year of having zero expenses. There are advantages to locating in the provinces besides the low cost of such operations. The quality of life away from the overcrowded capitals can be greater, and a typical paucity of local job opportunities with foreign corporations means that there is often a greater selection of highly qualified and enthusiastic staff available in the regions than in the capital. In Europe, employees' perceived quality of life frequently comes before salary in terms of evaluating job offers, and once people have grown out of their twenties and decided to start a family, there is a desire to move away from the capital city so they can have a house with a garden and not have to park their car on the street!

When setting up a new European office, decide what factors are critical for its success, and look at a regional location first.

Value Added Taxes—Do Not Forget to Reclaim Them!

The concept that a sales tax could be an asset on the balance sheet in the form of a receivable is alien to most American trained accountants. But in Europe, the Value Added Tax, their "sales tax," can be just such a receivable. Because of the nature of the tax, VAT is not much of a burden to most European businesses. VAT is an indirect tax charged on the value of most goods and services bought and sold, including rent and professional fees. Besides being charged at different rates on different goods and services—frequently utilities and food are exempt—different countries charge different rates, and cross border transactions may be taxable in one jurisdiction but not another.

It is therefore necessary to keep very detailed records in order to satisfy the numerous tax authorities and be in compliance with each country's rates and exemptions.

But the most important definitions to understand in terms of maximizing your company's profitability are "input tax" and "output tax." All VAT paid by a company on its own purchases is known as "Input VAT" and becomes an offset against VAT charged to customers— the "Output VAT." If Output is greater than Input, then the difference between the two is to be remitted to tax authorities. If the opposite is true, then the company receives a refund of the difference. Keeping track of all inputs is critical, because while a VAT auditor will demand that all your sales invoices charge VAT at the appropriate rate, he is unlikely to go through your purchase invoices to find offsets for you! At a 22 percent rate, failing to keep track of the tax on your purchases is a huge loss of profits.

I have seen too many instances where US companies have short changed themselves. In some cases, the European arm is "so small" that invoicing has taken place from the office of a US Controller. In others, the European division is "so large" that an American "shared services" department has sent out customer invoices and accounted for purchases "because the transaction cost per invoice" has allegedly been minimized by this shared service facility! But what each of these situations missed, because the assumption of their US centric accounting staff was that "a sales tax is a sales tax," was failure to treat the Input VAT as a receivable. Instead, they treated it as a cost of goods sold, an expense—inflating the costs of outside purchases by 20 percent or more! Assuming that in a typical company, purchases of outside services represents 30 percent of the company's expenses, correcting this error can increase gross margin by 6 percent. If a company is only making a 10 percent overall profit, this one action alone can increase the bottom line by 60 percent. Wow!

Learn everything you can about VAT.

Transfer Pricing

The profession you choose can say a lot about your personality, and there are more than enough jokes about introverted accountants. Cost accountants will diligently attempt to calculate the costs of anything produced to three significant digits. Salesmen rarely care about the cost of anything. But within an international corporate tax structure, these two personalities need to work together. Because of a concept known as transfer pricing, it is critical that when goods and services, intellectual property, management, and money are being transferred between foreign legal entities, that someone has calculated, validated and documented what is the most appropriate cost.

This is because in an era when governments worldwide are strapped for cash, and corporations don't vote, tax authorities are going after international corporations very aggressively in an effort to make them pay their "fair share." What this means in practice is that the US authorities will be trying to "prove" that you are selling your goods and services too cheaply to your overseas subsidiaries. The foreign authorities, in contrast, will take the opposite approach and look at those same goods and services and claim that you are raping and pillaging your foreign subsidiaries with ridiculously high prices.

In order to avoid long and drawn out battles with tax authorities, it is therefore critical that your transfer pricing policy is well thought out in advance, justifiable, applied consistently throughout ALL of your foreign subsidiaries, documented and acted on. Then, when you become the subject of an audit, you will be able to defend yourself, and if necessary, go all the way to competent authority. If you fail in any of these steps, you can assume that you will lose tax audits on both sides of the ocean, and effectively condemn yourself to double taxation. Why run the risk, when a well documented plan will lead to a successful landing?

Conclude an Advance Pricing Agreement before you engage in substantial intercompany international transactions.

Conclusion

While you may like to think that the way you do business in America is the best and only way to run a company, turning a blind eye to the actual way in which business is conducted overseas can cost you 10 to 20 percent of revenues on a recurring basis, and many millions of dollars if you don't plan appropriately. It is critical to ask questions and not blindly assume that our way is their way. There is a significant advantage in having as a CFO someone who has worked overseas and can assimilate all the different methodologies to maximize the bottom line impact. Competent international financial knowledge can impact the bottom line as significantly, or more, than an increase in revenues alone.

CHAPTER 14

Tying It All Together— The Successful Landing

Nothing satisfies me more at the end of an instrument flight than to descend through the clouds on the approach to an airport and see the runway lights straight in front of me. If the entire flight has been in the clouds, I still get a thrill that after many hours of seeing nothing but white outside the windshield, and watching little round dials and a purple line on a GPS, that the intended destination is in sight.

But why should seeing a runway straight ahead surprise me? If I have done everything that I should have, and there has been no mechanical malfunction en route, the outcome was planned. Failure was not an option!

And so it will be in your company. *Failure Is Not An Option* has provided you with examples of how successful companies allowed themselves to get into trouble in the first place, and shown you the remedies that were taken to enable them to become profitable once more. The stories chosen were by no means the only examples of failures at companies, they were just the most egregious. And while we restricted chapters on various expense classifications to the most likely to offer instant savings opportunities, the principles described apply to every aspect of the company.

The most critical action to be conveyed by top management, *is the mission*, to be shared by all who participate. If any member of the team does not believe in the survivability of the company, they should not be part of the team. All members of the executive team should be as one, and they should expect the same of their lieutenants. Success must become the new corporate mantra.

With the vision of a successful landing imparted to all employees, specific financial goals must be created. These are documented in the *13-Week Cash Flow Forecast*, the living, breathing document carried by the CFO at all times to reflect changes to the financial position of the company as they occur in real time. This document provides in clear detail where money is hemorrhaging from the company and the expense areas to focus on first.

Typically, this will involve staffing, and loss-making companies usually have more staff and pay more overtime than the business volumes require. Hand-in-hand with the cash flow forecast comes the *Organization Chart du Jour*, itself a living document to reflect staff changes as new policies are introduced to eliminate overtime, and curb non-productive behaviors.

Getting money in the door is critical when conventional sources of funding are drying up, or the bank is foreclosing on its loans because of breach of covenants. Receivables management must be a top priority. You must collect what is owed to you in a timely manner. This has two major benefits—it means that your working capital requirements decline, and the chances for debts to go bad are significantly reduced. Preventing bad debts in a typical company can have the same effect on profits as a sales increase of seven percent.

In the chapter on benefits, examples were provided describing opportunities for both the employer and the employee to save by changing the mix of benefits on offer and creating tax advantaged methods of paying for them.

We also showed how reconciliations and controls play a big part in reducing expenditures. What gets measured gets done. It was revealed how there is a high likelihood that you are overpaying your third party benefits administrator for existing benefits, and that such overpayment will be found through reconciliations. Likewise, later in the book, we showed how failing to analyze gross margins, and failing to reconcile volumes of products purchased to volumes sold allowed corrupt employees to sell product for cash.

Advance planning plays its part in a number of areas of cost reduction. Requiring at least a one week advance purchase for all airline tickets, buying them and traveling on mid-week days, and forbidding any travel which does not meet that requirement will reduce domestic airline costs by two-thirds. Controlling what travelers pay for a trip, rather than whether they go on the trip is critical because numerous studies have shown that companies whose employees travel are more successful than those who don't. So we say, *Travel and Entertainment—Yes!*, but accomplish much more by spending much less.

If you are in the transportation business, planning applies to selecting routes well in advance to ensure that customers are not passed en-route to others without themselves receiving a delivery. This can take 20 percent off your delivery costs.

Managing the risks of an airplane flight involves checking weather, the plane itself, the pilot's familiarity with the plane, the route and the pilot's own general health. The FAA requires that before a flight, the pilot *"familiarize himself with all available information,"* a tall order in today's information age, but all encompassing. By being situationally aware and prepared, the chances of a successful landing are higher than if you took off into the wild blue yonder without any idea of where you were going or how you were going to get there. In your own company, risk management in the form of who you hire, how you train them, and the culture of safety and care within the organization can have a dramatic, as much as 50 percent impact on insurance rate reduction.

Other professional fees need to be managed as well—pay the outside auditors and attorneys for advice only they are capable of providing because of their many years of experience. Don't pay an outside CPA $200 per hour to produce decent supporting documents for the audit when you might be able to hire part-time clerical help for 80 percent less. Likewise, you don't need a high priced associate attorney charging for basic research your own administrative assistant could perform.

Banks as well as lawyers are always the butt of jokes, but you need to get serious with your banking relationship, making the bank work for you rather than the other way round. Consolidate your loans, open a sweep account, and if the opportunity exists, take out a line of credit simply to take advantage of vendors you have which offer the opportunity to take a two percent discount for prompt payment.

Gross margin analysis is the source of many treasure troves in companies. Not only will detailed analysis of what occurs to what was expected highlight weaknesses in the existing plan, requiring mid-course corrections, it will also identify opportunities for fraud. Taken to its logical extreme, profitability analysis will be extended to reviewing ROI on investment projects, as well as to more detailed analysis such as Customer Profitability.

It is highly likely that a contributing factor to a company's under-performance is a tolerance for waste and profligacy. This is often demonstrated in a transportation department which does not manage fuel consumption by vehicle or driver, and truck fleets left idling for hours at a time instead of being switched off. Controlling this visible waste of resources sends a message to everyone in the company that waste *will not* be tolerated. The message can be extended to turning off lights, eliminating unnecessary office equipment, recycling paper etc. In the case of office supplies, the dollars saved may not be as significant as the message communicated that we care about our efficient use of resources so that we can provide the customer the best possible price for our services.

One of the most satisfying ways to reduce costs is to reduce your tax burden. Always verify that you are not overstating your assets, and that if there are alternative methods of calculating a tax due, you work them all and submit the most favorable. If you have international operations, always assume that the tax methodologies will be different, and even though you may consider some of them farcical, ask out-of-the-box questions. You may find some totally unexpected ways to reduce overseas tax. Always plan your transfer pricing in advance and structure your operations so that if losses are expected for business reasons, that those losses are not trapped in a far flung jurisdiction with no fiscal benefit elsewhere in the organization.

And also remember, with foreign operations, you do not need to be in the Capital City or its environs. In many countries, costs of doing business near the Capital may be three times higher than in the provinces. And as your international advisors may not always put your interests ahead of their own, ensure that you have on your own staff, someone who has traveled around the world and can temper the advice provided from overseas and separate fact from fiction.

Finally, remember that the journey never ends. To keep the plane in the air when it is being buffeted by extreme turbulence requires focusing on just six instruments to keep it right side up at a speed low enough to prevent break-up. At that point in the flight, nothing else matters. Likewise in your company, if bankruptcy is looming, your only objective is to live another week with enough cash. Gross margin analysis can wait! So set your priorities and turn around your business. *Failure Is Not An Option* provides you all the navigation charts you need to accomplish that successful landing.

"Another successful landing, Captain!"

APPENDIX 1

Checklist for Calculation of Expected Savings
Obtainable by Implementing "Failure Is Not An Option"

MANUFACTURING COMPANY INCOME STATEMENT	REVENUE/ EXPENSE	% SAVINGS ESTIMATE	DOLLARS SAVED
REVENUES	50,000,000		
EXPENSES			
MATERIALS (40% of of sales price)	20,000,000	2	400,000
WAGES AND SALARIES (Base - 250 employees at $64k/yr)	16,000,000	2	320,000
OVERTIME (120 emps, 8 hrs/wk, $40/hr)	2,000,000	100	2,000,000
BENEFITS (250 employees at $9,600/yr)	2,400,000	2	48,000
BAD DEBT WRITE OFFS (2% of revenues)	1,000,000	100	1,000,000
REDUCTION OF DAYS SALES OUTSTANDING (From 120 to 40 at 8% interest)			880,000
INTEREST EXPENSE ($4m loan, $3m net debt at 8%)	320,000	25	80,000
TRAVEL AND ENTERTAINMENT	4,000,000	50	2,000,000
PROFESSIONAL FEES	400,000	20	80,000
INSURANCE	500,000	25	125,000
TRANSPORTATION	480,000	30	144,000
PROPERTY, SALES AND USE, FRANCHISE TAXES	500,000	25	125,000
RENT	1,200,000	10	120,000
OTHER OFFICE EXPENSES	1,200,000	15	180,000
TOTALS	50,000,000		7,502,000

HOW A $50 MILLION REVENUE COMPANY CAN INCREASE PROFITS BY $7.5 MILLION

217

APPENDIX 2

Checklist for Getting Started

THE FOLLOWING ACCOUNTING RECORDS SHOULD BE AVAILABLE FOR REVIEW

Corporate Organization, Subsidiaries

Annual (audited) Financial Statements For Last 3 Years

Monthly Financial Statements For Last 12 Months

Detailed General Ledger

Employee List

Organization Chart

Total amounts of compensation paid, classified as wages, overtime, benefits

Benefit Plans

Aged Receivables Ledger—by Customer

Details of all bad debts written off in last 2 years

Aged Payables Ledger

Details of all Bank Accounts

Loan Agreements

Details of all Travel and Entertaining, by Employee

Details of all Professional fees

Insurance Policies

All Insurance Claims Last Five Years

Rental Agreements

Fixed Asset Ledger

Tax Invoices for Personal Property, Delaware Franchise

APPENDIX 3

APPENDIX 3, SHEET 1

TURNAROUND COMPANY INC CASH FLOW SUMMARY - MOVING 13 WEEK AVERAGE   **SHEET 1 - REVENUE FORECAST**

Date of Most Recent Update - January 3

	Jan	Feb	Mar
Monthly Revenues	3291	3987	3912
Monthly Payments	4196 (5 weeks - includes 3 payrolls)	3595	3429

Week Beginning	Jan 1	Jan 8	Jan 15	Jan 22	Jan 29	Feb 5	Feb 12	Feb 19	Feb 26	Mar 5
Opening A/R balance, start of week	7230	7638	7068	7431	7275	7551	7038	6688	7049	6902
Net Revenes from sub total below (source VP Sales Forecast as adjusted)	558	540	813	600	780	579	1056	996	1356	696
Customer 1 - France										
Customer 2	30	30	30	30	30					
Customer 3	300	300	300	300	300					
Customer 4			33			246	246	246	246	246
Customer 5	138									
Customer 6 - Denmark		120		180		33				
Customer 7										
Customer 8 - Dubai			360		360		360		360	
Service Contracts/Recurring revenues	90	90	90	90	90	150	150	150	150	150
Not yet identified						150	300	600	600	300
TOTAL REVENUES THIS WEEK/MONTH	558	540	813	600	780	579	1056	996	1356	696
Collections (from next sheet)	-150	-1110	-450	-756	-504	-1092	-1406	-635	-1503	-750
Closing A/R balance - end of week	7638	7068	7431	7275	7551	7038	6688	7049	6902	6848

APPENDIX 3

APPENDIX 3, SHEET 2

TURNAROUND COMPANY INC CASH FLOW SUMMARY - MOVING 13 WEEK AVG **SHEET 2 - RECEIVABLES COLLECTIONS AND CASH AVAILABILITY**

Week Beginning	CUSTOMER RECEIVABLE actual dollars At December 31	Jan 1	Jan 8	Jan 15	Jan 22	Jan 29	Feb 5	Feb 12	Feb 19	Feb 26	Mar 5
Cash Balance at start of week/month		1000	-25	720	31	420	-226	254	487	640	814
Collections:											
Customer 1 - France	360,000										
Customer 2	534,324				240	54		20			
Customer 3	2,147,418		600	240	240						
Customer 4	469,452			120			600			600	
Customer 5	557,628						348				
Customer 6 - Denmark	237,726		180				54				
Customer 7	136,632				102				5		
Customer 8 - Dubai	586,338				84			498			
Previous Customer	960,000		240					720			
Previous Customer	441,378	60				360		78			
Previous Customer	37,974										
From Recurring Revenues	261,012	90	90	90	90	90	90	90	90	90	150
Total collectible receivables	**6,729,882**										
From New Customers 6 weeks after sale									540	813	600
Total Collections		150	1110	450	756	504	1092	1406	635	1503	750
Total Cash Available		1150	1085	1170	787	924	866	1660	1122	2143	1564

APPENDIX 3

APPENDIX 3, SHEET 3

TURNAROUND COMPANY INC CASH FLOW SUMMARY - MOVING 13 WEEK AVERAGE

SHEET 3 - SUMMARY EXPENSE CLASSIFICATIONS

Week Beginning	Jan 1	Jan 8	Jan 15	Jan 22	Jan 29	Feb 5	Feb 12	Feb 19	Feb 26	Mar 5
Materials	223	216	325	240	312	232	422	398	542	278
Payroll - bi-weekly	540		540		540		530		530	
Overtime	38	38	20	20	10	5	5			
Employee Benefits	120		120		120		100		100	
Sales Commissions	30		30		30		30		30	
Outside Contractors	15	15	10	15	5					
Travel and Entertainment	60	60	58	56	54	52	50	48	46	45
Office Rent						240				240
Utilities	12	12	12	12	12	12	12	12	12	12
Insurance	12					12				12
Professional Fees						30				
Trade Shows/Marketing						5				5
Operating Leases - Copiers, etc.	6	6	6	6	6	6	6	6	5	5
Small Furniture/Repairs and Maintenance	6	6	6	6	6	6	6	6	5	5
Office Supplies	12	12	12	12	12	12	12	12	10	10
CAPEX									5	5
Bank Charges	60				2				2	
Interest on $1m Loan - $33k repayments begin Jan 31	41				41				41	
Total Payments	1175	365	1139	367	1150	612	1173	482	1328	617
Closing Cash End Of Week	-25	720	31	420	-226	254	487	640	814	947

APPENDIX 4

Sample Travel and Entertainment (T+E) Policy

Overall Goal of Company's Travel and Entertainment Policy:

- How to do more with less—the key is planning.

This document discusses the expectations, guidelines and reporting requirements for employees required to travel on company business.

Expectations

Employees are adults with personal preferences. Travel can be perceived by different people as a benefit of or a detractor to the job. Travel undertaken without adequate planning of both the journey and its objectives can waste significant resources, whereas well-planned travel can enable the company to achieve revenue gains and strategic objectives.

Travel is necessary, and even though air travel these days is onerous, it should be relatively pleasant, safe, and convenient. However, it should also be conducted in the most cost-effective manner, in order to safeguard the profitability of the company, and the security of employment for all staff.

This means first and foremost that all out of town meetings be planned sufficiently far in advance that advantage can be taken of advance purchase discounts on airfares, and that multiple calls can be made in the same town on one trip, rather than making multiple trips over successive weeks to the same town.

It is understood that meeting schedules often change, but our company policy is that WE do not change meetings, once on the calendar. Therefore, we would expect the same courtesy from the people we meet. We must communicate this to our meeting partners and request that they understand that we will be incurring expenses in advance of our meetings and that cancellation will cost us money. While we cannot prevent them from cancelling meetings, what we can do is limit the amount of rescheduling we do to accommodate a client, as this "early" behavior is indicative of the way they will treat the relationship going forward.

The purpose of this document is to create a fair, reasonable and logical T+E policy, which takes account of employee preferences, and describe how it will be administered.

The overall goal is to accomplish the necessary business objectives at the lowest overall practical cost.

Guidelines

All travel must be planned and booked at least one week in advance in order to obtain lowest advance purchase rates.

All expenses reasonably incurred by the employee in furtherance of the business objectives will be reimbursed by the company on presentation of the appropriate documentation.

All T+E reimbursement requests should be considered as if the documents were available to all employees to review.

Air

Choice of airline is a very personal affair, and most people have a loyalty to a particular airline. Employees have a free choice of airline, provided that loyalty for the purposes of generating points does not cost the company more than an independent decision would cost. Low cost carriers such as *Frontier, Jet Blue* and *Southwest* serve many markets and typically have the lowest fares. Legacy carriers usually meet these fares when they have flights at similar times. The fares offered by these low cost carriers will be the benchmarks against which actual fares paid are reviewed, so if your selection of fare is significantly greater than that offered by an LCC, your reimbursement may be questioned.

Employees are expected to be familiar with airline websites, so they can review all options available for travel to a specific location. Our designated travel expert is "X" who will gladly assist travelers who may want some additional guidance regarding specific web sites.

All travel must be purchased at least one week in advance, unless there are special sales which match advance purchase rates. All tickets purchased must be non-refundable, flight-specific tickets.

Prior to purchasing a ticket, consideration must be given to:

Day of week and time of day
Prices can vary 500 percent for the same journey for departures within a few hours of each other.

Nearby cities
Driving to a large hub such as Dallas or Chicago and driving the last 100 miles may be 75 percent less expensive than flying direct to Waco or Milwaukee.

Day of the Week to Purchase Ticket
Avoid purchasing tickets on a Sunday—the airline systems are usually trying out how high they can price fares for the new week. Try to buy on a Tuesday when the specials are usually released.

Segments not Round-Trips
Most airlines now price one way tickets at half the price of round trip tickets. If there are no savings to be obtained by buying a round trip or multi city ticket, always buy separate segments, so that in the unlikely event you have to change partial plans, only one half of the ticket will be wasted.

International Travel to Continental Europe
For travelers authorized to use business class, there is a maximum fare allowed of $4,000 round trip. Always consider flying to a UK

secondary airport such as Manchester, Birmingham, Glasgow, or Edinburgh and taking a low cost carrier from there to Europe, as such pricing will usually be 50% - 60% less than the cost of flying direct from the US to Paris or Frankfurt.

Segments within Europe

Be aware that EasyJet (*www.easyjet.com*) is the largest airline within Europe and is comfortable, reliable, and inexpensive, as are FlyBe, and AirBerlin. These airlines should be your first choice for flights within Europe. Their tickets can only be purchased on the web. Also consider intercity trains whose tickets can be purchased on *www.raileurope.com.*

Hotel

Safety and comfort in a quiet room are our prime concerns. Ostentation is not appropriate. In today's environment, clients would rather we spend our money wisely rather than wildly. You should select hotels which offer free Internet. Hampton, Hilton Garden Inn and Sheraton all provide good value.

Hotels should be appropriate for the business being conducted, and be safe, clean and comfortable. Unless all meetings are being conducted downtown, out of town hotels should be considered, especially if they offer free parking.

AAA discounts should be utilized.

Car Rental

The company has complimentary *Hertz Gold, Alamo Emerald Isle* and *Avis Wizard* memberships for employees so that pick up and drop off is quick and easy. The company will not reimburse for add-ons such as insurance (covered by the company's liability policy), never lost, or fuel refill option. These options can often double or triple the cost of a rental, for very little benefit. You are expected to refill the car yourself prior to its return.

Meals

Business entertaining is important and expected. The quality and value of the restaurant should match the expected benefit from the meeting. Expensive bottles of wine are inappropriate and may be perceived as a negative by a prospective buyer who knows that such extravagance will be built into the cost of the product he might be buying.

Airport Transportation and Parking

You will be reimbursed for one round trip to the airport per business trip, calculated as the number of miles round trip from our office to the airport at the prevailing IRS rate, plus the number of nights parking at the economy lot rate. You may choose any means of transport to the airport, but your reimbursement will always be at the above rate.

Administration

All T+E reports are to be submitted to the CFO for the periods ended the 15th and 31st of the month, within one week of the cut-off date, approved by your direct supervisor. All claims for reimbursement must be supported by appropriate documentation, and the dates reflect the actual dates of travel. This means that an airfare for travel on April 1st should be submitted with the T+E report for April 1st. A round trip ticket should be submitted for full reimbursement with the T+E report for the date the trip started.

General Exceptions to Reimbursements

Note that reimbursement will not be made for expenses which are greater than they would be if the employee were making the same trip for personal reasons such as:

- Purchasing the most expensive airline ticket rather than picking a travel time which would minimize cost.

- Using a limo to get to the airport.

- If self driving to the airport, parking in the covered close-in garage rather than the remote surface lot.

- Spending lavishly on food and drink at the airport and on the plane.

- Staying at a hotel significantly more expensive than usual.

- Using valet parking to save a couple of minutes walk.

- Dining alone at the best steak house in town.

- Renting in room movies.

Conclusion

This policy is subject to change and at all times, best professional judgment is the guiding principle.

APPENDIX 5
Sample Receivables Collections Policy

The overall guiding principle is to avoid any bad debt write off. In a typical company, it takes five new sales to make up for one write off. Prompt collections actions can prevent write offs. Finance will work collaboratively with Sales to ensure all accounts are collected. Sales commissions are paid only on collected accounts.

New Customer Set Up

Before an order can be shipped, the following information must be provided by the salesman to create a new customer account:

Shipping information
- Physical address (Any restrictions on time of deliveries?)
- Recipient's name and title
- Recipient's phone number

Billing information
- Mailing address
- Name and title to whom invoice should be sent
- Phone number of invoice recipient

Invoicing

Invoices will be created as soon as practical from shipping documents. Invoices will clearly state terms of payment, normally within 30 days of date of invoice.

New customers will be contacted by the Accounts Receivable clerk within one week of mailing the invoice to confirm that it has been received by the appropriate person. The customer will be asked to verify that everything appears correct with regard to the amounts owed.

Collection

If payment has not been received by 30 days from date of invoice, the customer will be contacted by phone to ascertain the reasons why not. If valid reasons are provided, such as incorrect delivery, poor quality, service or follow up, the A/R Clerk will work with other staff in the company to rectify the issue so that ultimate collection is not jeopardized.

The CFO and salesman will be notified for information that the customer has not met the terms of payment and the reasons why.

Once the ostensible reason for non-payment has been rectified, the A/R Clerk will maintain frequent communication with the customer, making detailed notes of each conversation, so that the customer is aware that we take payment seriously.

Any indications perceived by the A/R Clerk that collection is in jeopardy will be communicated immediately to the CFO.

If the invoice remains unpaid for a further 30 days after "issues" have been rectified, the CFO may elect to put the customer's account on hold.

APPENDIX 6

Research on Drug Free Workplaces

Cost to Employers of Employees with a Diagnosed Chemical Dependency Problem:

- Alcoholism causes 500 million lost workdays each year. (6)

Alcoholics are expensive to businesses in several different ways:

- Workplace accident rates are two or three times higher than normal;
- Alcoholics are five times more likely to file a worker's compensation claim; and
- Alcoholics are 2.5 times more likely to have absences of eight days or more. (5)

Employees diagnosed with a chemical dependency problem in a large manufacturing plant were found to have:

- Six times the number of absences;
- Higher incidence of injuries, hypertension, and mental disorders. (7)

References

1. Hoffman, J.P.; Brittingham, A.; and Larison, C. (1996). *Drug use among U.S. workers: Prevalence and trends by occupation and industry categories. Number DHH S Publ. No. (SM A) 96 - 30 89. Rockville, MD: SAMHSA, Office of Applied Studies.*
2. French, M.T.; Zarkin, G.A.; Hartwell, T.D.; and Bray, J.W. (1995). Prevalence and consequences of smoking, alcohol use, and illicit drug use at five worksites. *Public Health Rep. 110:593 - 599.*
3. Hoffman, J.P.; Larison , C.; and Sanderson, A. (1997). *An analysis of worker drug use and workplace policies and programs. Rockville, MD, Substance Abuse and Mental Health Services Administration, Office of Applied Studies,* A - 2 Analytic Series.

4. National Household Survey on Drug Abuse: Main Findings 1991 (1993). Substance Abuse and Mental Health Services Administration, Rockville, MD.

5. "Drug abuse in the workplace: An employer's guide for prevention." *EAP Digest.*

6. Department of Labor. (1998). "Working partners for an alcohol - and drug-free American workplace," (hep://www.dol.gov/dol/asp).

7. Bross, M.H.; Pace, S.K.; and Cronin, I.H. (1992). Chemical dependence: Analysis of work absenteeism and associated mental illness. *Journal of Occupational Medicine 34(1):1 6-19.*

8. Greenberg, E.S.; and Grunberg, L. (1995). Work alienation and problem alcohol behavior. *Journal of Health and Social Behavior 36(1):83-1102.*

9. Delaney, W.P. and Ames, G. (1995). Work team attitudes, drinking norms, and work place drinking. The *Journal of Drug Issues 25(2): 275-290.*

APPENDIX 7

Fuel Conservation No Idle Matter at UPS

Press Release - June 14, 2006 11:17 AM

You wouldn't think of something as benign as avoiding a left-hand turn could conserve fuel, but Atlanta-based United Parcel Service (UPS) swears by it. In fact, the parcel carrier has technology in its systems that help map out routes that minimize the number of left turns the driver has to make. According to spokesperson Steve Holmes, avoiding left turns at intersections reduces idling which in turn lowers fuel consumption. "It seems small, but when you multiply it across 88,000 vehicles making nearly 15 million deliveries every day during the course of a year, it adds up."

And at stop lights, making a right turn at an intersection tends to be faster than a left turn, since you have only to wait for an opportunity to turn into one lane of traffic. You also have the option of "right on red" in most jurisdictions, unless otherwise indicated by traffic signs. "So even if you didn't save fuel, you're going to move more quickly through a route."

"Because 98 percent of our packages are processed electronically by shippers, we know what's entering our system each day, what's still in our system each day, when each package is going to arrive at a center, when the package is scheduled for delivery—including time of day— and where it will be delivered," Holmes says.

What's more, Holmes says, UPS drivers are trained to always turn off their package trucks when they stop for a delivery, never idling at the curb or in a driveway. "Even if the driver is out of the truck for a few seconds, the vehicle is always turned off."

ABOUT THE AUTHOR

Philip Varley is an internationally acclaimed turn-around expert who has worked in more than twenty countries on six continents. His relentless pursuit of financial management excellence has enabled him to turn around eight companies in the last twenty years. These businesses have ranged in size from small chemicals distributors, software and consulting firms, and privately owned metals manufacturers, to large international publicly quoted companies.

The techniques he uses to maximize profits are described in detail in this book, and if you follow them, you should be able to achieve a typical cost reduction in excess of 10 percent.

Varley graduated from Imperial College, London, with a degree in Chemical Engineering, and then qualified as a Chartered Accountant. Combining engineering with finance, he joined Arthur Andersen's London Office, where his most unusual experiences included re-supplying a drilling rig in the North Sea, and working as a contractor for a US oil company in a troubled Middle Eastern country, reconciling oil production reports and royalty payments.

In 1985, he emigrated to the US and obtained his MBA from the University of Denver. He qualified as a CPA and spent three years with Ersnt and Whinney as an Audit Manager, during which time he uncovered a fraud at a defense contractor and performed a number of due diligence analyses for UK companies investing in the US.

As the International Controller for a NASDAQ traded software company, his most significant achievement was the restructuring of the European operations, saving over $4 million in taxes. He also became a transfer pricing expert and won a $3 million judgment at Competent Authority. Subsequently as the Divisional Finance Director for a Fortune 100 company, he increased profits by more than $11 million.

During the Internet boom of the late 1990s, he was instrumental in raising over $50 million of equity for three start-ups, two of which were acquired. The understanding of the factors leading to these successes led Varley to his current role, concentrating his efforts on improving what already exists at current clients. He does this by taking a laser-like focus to every single line item in a company's operation, understanding the financial implications of the decisions, and expanding that analysis into general management technique. The result is a successful turnaround.

Philip Varley's "12-Step Plan" described in *Failure Is Not An Option* utilizes two critical documents, the *13-Week Cash Flow Forecast*, and the *Organizational Chart du Jour*. Combining these two pieces of paper to create his play book, he takes a methodical approach to maximizing an organization's profitability by removing dead wood, demonstrating from his myriad experiences how to do more with less, and growing a cadre of excited and focused management and staff.

Adding to the unique and insightful experiences described in this book, Varley's love of multi-cultural experiences has led him to travel the world visiting 83 countries on all seven continents. When at home in Colorado, he enjoys climbing Colorado's 14ers, skiing, or flying his Cessna over the mountains. He is currently working on his next book, a photo essay entitled *Colorado's 14ers From the Air*.

Philip Varley can be contacted at:
PV@TheBGI.com
303-946-1941
1 Mountain Cedar Lane, Denver, CO 80127
www.TheBGI.com